WHEN LINES ARE DRAWN

A GUIDE TO
RESOLVING CONFLICT
IN THE CHURCH

WHEN LINES ARE DRAWN

A GUIDE TO RESOLVING CONFLICT IN THE CHURCH

E. STEVE EIDSON

COLLEGE PRESS
PUBLISHING COMPANY
Joplin, Missouri

International Standard Book Number 0-89900-685-X
Library of Congress Catalog Card Number: 94-72127

TABLE OF CONTENTS

INTRODUCTION

This book has been born out of conflict: intrapersonal conflict as the willful nature of man has striven against the will of a righteous God, and interpersonal conflict as individuals have differed on values, goals, and methods. Literally, this book has been born out of the waters of a flood, where people fought against the worst natural disaster of the state of Georgia and lost.

Yet, out of each aspect of the birth process, individuals have found new life in Christ, the kingdom of God has advanced, and out of the flood waters a stronger congregation is emerging. Such can be the nature of conflict.

The goal of this book is twofold. First, to provide help in understanding the inner workings of conflict. Second, with a better understanding of conflict's nature in place, to help reduce the fear that arises when conflict occurs. Growth, personal and corporate, does not come without struggle. In one sense, we should welcome that struggle, allowing God to use it for our growth and his glory.

CHAPTER 1

LINES IN THE DIRT

It was a gorgeous spring day. The playground seemed normal enough. Recess was going on with a fervor that only children can provide. The swings were being used, a line had formed for the slide, and a softball game was reaching the excitement level of the world series. But all was not well.

In the group of children awaiting their turn to bat, a disagreement was occurring that would ultimately spoil the rest of the day for at least two boys. One boy slipped into line ahead of another but was pushed aside by the latter, with the result that both squared off ready to do battle. An argument ensued where each forcefully stated his position. "I missed my turn last inning," the first stated. "Tough luck," the second sneered. "You can just wait until I get my turn!" After several exchanges the second boy with a flourish dragged his foot in the dirt, making a line and daring the first to step across. With a leap the first crossed the line, tackled the other, and, as boys are prone to do, proceeded to do little damage. Outside the principal's office as they wrote for the 500th time, "I will not fight on the playground," both boys came to realize the foolishness of their actions and their friendship was restored.

We smile at the actions of children, but isn't it strange that as adults we still revert to childish ways. How many "lines in the dirt" have been drawn during family conversations, in church leadership meetings, in negotiations between union and management officials, or in relationships with friends? Each of us has stepped across the line drawn by another. Possibly the step was taken unknowingly, but in some instances the commitment to our own position was the motivating factor. Just as real are the lines that we scuff in the dirt that express the boundaries that another person may not cross.

CONSEQUENCES OF CONFLICT

The consequences of either party stepping across the line are far more serious than the writing of a few sentences. Strained relationships, hurt feelings, the depletion of a group's influence, or the emotional or physical separation of individuals can all occur. Nowhere are the consequences of unresolved conflict more evident and more destructive than in the life of the church. An atmosphere of tension that pervades even the worship services will repel newcomers. Church fights impede the witness of the church in a given community. Divided and split congregations water down any plea for unity. Individuals may leave the church or at best withdraw their support and service.

Undoubtedly, the most serious result of conflict can be the reality of individuals being lost for all eternity. Hank and his family were very active members of our congregation, Hank having served as a deacon and Sarah, his wife, working actively in the choir and ladies group. A recommendation was made to the congregation concerning the addition of classroom space to our building. During the interval between the recommendation being presented and the actual vote on the proposal, Hank was given incorrect information by an individual who had a long history of disgruntlement within the church.

Hank reacted to that information, would not allow anyone with the correct information to influence his thinking, and left the church. To this day Hank and his wife have not returned. Neither have they begun attending any other congregation. His family has had several crises in the last eleven years. They have suffered through those without the benefit of the support of Christ's body, even though it has been offered. Unless there is change, these folk, their abilities, witnesses, and their lives are lost to Christ and his church.

The issues that are to be addressed in this book are not small and insignificant. We dare not approach the issue of conflict with a "Ho Hum, well, it really doesn't matter" attitude. In fact, the attitude of "well, we really ought to get along with each other better" does not go far enough. Beginning with church leadership and progressing throughout the body of Christ, we must work to learn to respond to conflict positively and constructively.

It is the purpose of the book to challenge Christians to deal with conflict constructively, to enable the leadership of the church to foster a climate where "crossing the line" will not produce the disasters normally associated with conflict. To begin to accomplish this, first of all, existing attitudes toward conflict itself must be explored.

ATTITUDES TOWARD CONFLICT

Negative Attitudes and Their Consequences

Myron Rush, in his book *Management: A Biblical Approach*, defines conflict as "open and hostile opposition occurring as a result of differing viewpoints."[1] He differentiates conflict from disagreement by stating that conflict always involves the expression of hostility while disagreement may be expressed without hostility. Rush further states that "conflict comes from our own selfish desires and passions. . .The objective is almost always to impose our ideas, beliefs, desires, and opinions on others."[2]

Even though Rush's attempt to separate conflict from disagreement at best is an attempt at semantic gymnastics, his statements about conflict do illustrate one attitude toward conflict: conflict equals sin. This view of conflict is one that is widely held within the church. McSwain and Treadwell point out in their book *Conflict Ministry in the Church*, "Organizational conflict is as real in the church as in any human organization. It is often dealt with less openly in the church, however, because of the basic feeling among many that disagreements and differences ought not occur among Christians."[3] It is not the fear that conflict will have destructive ends that causes church leaders to avoid disagreements at all costs, but the belief that conflict violates an unstated norm that such activity is a no-no and should be avoided.

11

When George invited John into his lumber business, most of their friends were very surprised. Their ages, interests, and philosophies of business were radically different. The only things they held in common were their church and fiery tempers. Obviously, no one was surprised when a few months later words and ultimately blows were exchanged.

When in just a few days the elders of their church realized that portions of the congregation were aligning themselves with the two primaries, a meeting was convened to discuss the response that was needed. Predictably the elders themselves were divided, each deploring the events that had ensued but feeling that possibly one or the other was less wrong in his actions.

Jim, the minister of the congregation, felt that in order for the unity of the congregation to be preserved as well as the lives of the two men, a definite attempt at mediation on the part of the elders was needed. The initial response of the elders was discouraging. The predominant feeling was one of hands off. "This is not our fight; we do not need to get involved," said one man. Another remarked, "We need to keep this under wraps as much as possible." "We need to stay out of this and let them sort this out," remarked a third.

This concept of conflict can also be seen in the attempts of church leaders to quell any disagreement, in censorious preaching against any who might openly disagree with a particular program, and within families when conflicts are ignored or kept under wraps. In each case the accepted idea is that if conflict is present, there must be sin in the camp.

The absence of conflict does not necessarily imply that all is well within any institution. There very well may be a marked lack of trust among people and an underlying fear that if feelings are expressed, the distance that is seen or felt among individuals might increase. Because of prior conflicts that have remained unresolved, the possibility exists that groups within the congregation feel powerless to either resolve the conflict or move the groups onward to new effectiveness in ministry.

By suppressing conflict rather than facing the real or imagined consequences of it, congregations expose themselves to an even greater danger. If not resolved, conflicts that have long been buried can erupt without warning in even greater measure. Willimon in *Preaching about Conflict in the Local Church* observes, "Where a congregation operates on a style of constant suppression of conflict, conflict acts like a pressure cooker. The heat continues to build; the inevitable explosion is more destructive."[4]

Positive Attitudes and Their Consequences

Robert Clinton, in contrast to Rush, sees conflict in an entirely different light. In his book *The Making of a Leader*, he states that "conflict is a powerful tool in the hand of God and can be used to teach a leader lessons that he would not learn in any other way."[5] For Clinton, conflict is a learning process that is crucial in the development of a leader within the church. He points out that "God will use conflict to point out areas of character needing modification, to point out or confirm areas of strength, or to point out areas of character entirely missing."[6]

If Clinton is correct in his assumption that conflict is used by God as a many-faceted teaching tool for leaders, it would also be possible to assume that God would use conflict in much the same way for the total church. McSwain and Treadwell point out that "conflict is most likely within families, business partnerships, groups with a lengthy history of personal care for individuals within it, and organizations which have fostered deep personal relationships. Conflict occurs most often in congregations in which there is a deep commitment to the church."[7] This deep commitment affects the world as they watch the church respond to serious problems. Willimon is correct when he says that "because the church is rightly judged by the character of the people who comprise the church, our response to conflict is part of our witness to the world that Jesus Christ makes possible a people who are able to live with one another in hope and peace."[8]

CONFLICT'S EFFECTS ON CONGREGATIONAL LIFE

The attitudes toward conflict that are adopted by church leadership will affect congregational life in many ways. It will first of all affect the way in which conflict is handled. When conflict is treated as sin, disagreements will be quickly squelched or covered over, communication will be discouraged, and those with whom we disagree will be labeled as sinful either consciously or unconsciously.

Don is an elder who does not like conflict. Each and every time there is a ripple of disagreement, Don launches into his sermonette that encourages agreement, reminding those within hearing of the need to work together and of the necessity of getting along. Many times the sheer volume of words that he offers has shamed individuals into agreement even though deep down they still maintain their positions.

Brad, also an elder, sees every question that is directed at the eldership as a challenge to their authority. He is very quick to remind the questioner that the elders are responsible for the oversight of the congregation and have been given that authority by God. Conflict is stopped dead in its tracks, at least on the surface. There is a rising undercurrent in Brad's congregation that very well may swell into a tidal wave of dissatisfaction.

If, on the other hand, conflict is seen as a productive tool of God, then the expression of opposing viewpoints will be encouraged, honest communication of ideas will be heard, and labels will not be attached to individuals. This can be seen in our experience with Mrs. Blair.

Mrs. Blair, 88 years old, somewhat hard of hearing, and as a result of that, somewhat loud in her speech, sat on the back row of the sanctuary during a congregational meeting. The purpose of that meeting was to vote on a resolution that would enable us to double the size of the sanctuary. Mrs. Blair had been somewhat vocal in her opposition to the project in the days when it was being discussed and had openly communicated that to several of the church's leaders, myself included. Each of us had listened to her arguments, had disagreed with her in our conversations, but to a man listened and encouraged her to talk to others if that was her wish.

Now in the meeting as she listened to the many questions that were being asked, she turned, caught my attention, and motioned me to come over behind her. Somewhat apprehensive, I moved over to her and almost fainted as I heard her words. "I don't understand what all the ruckus is about. It seems like you guys finally have got your ducks together. Let's get on with it!"

She spoke these words in an increasing volume and finally every one else became quiet. "It seems that Mrs. Blair has something to say," someone remarked. "No, not at all," she replied. The individual presiding immediately responded, "Blair, we've listened to everything else you have said; we aren't going to stop now." Following that comment, she did share with the rest the comment she had made to me with a little extra. Following her speech, the motion was made and seconded for the resolution's adoption, and it passed by a 98% margin.

She had been heard, even though there was initial disagreement with an idea. That hearing provided her with the opportunity to express her feelings, but much more than that, she was given the opportunity to listen to others as well. The free and open exchange of thoughts and ideas enabled her to see a well-thought-out opportunity to expand the ministry of our congregation, not a half-baked idea as she originally thought.

The second way that the life of a congregation will be affected is in the results of conflict. If the expressed attitude toward conflict is negative, the hurts and feelings of individuals can be ignored; conflicts can remain unresolved only to erupt at a later time with even more serious consequences; and the growth pattern of a congregation or an individual can be stymied.

"If we had just taken care of this two years ago, this would not have happened." This general comment was agreed upon by the four men sitting around the dining room table. As elders of the church, they had seen their congregation gradually lose momentum, stagnate, and finally erupt in a flash of harsh feelings at that morning's congregational meeting. What was the cause?

About two years ago, several criticisms were heard of the minister who admittedly was getting up in years and was somewhat forgetful. But he was unwilling to recognize this and was very dogmatic in his denial that certain events and situations had occurred. The elders at that time felt that the minister's retirement was imminent and so made no response to the complaints. The minister's wife suddenly became ill and after a short illness passed away. Several questions were asked by individuals within the congregation as to what the minister planned to do. His wife's death completely devastated him and for several months he was able to function only at a minimal level within the congregation. Many tasks remained undone, and while being sympathetic to his situation, many began to openly criticize the state of affairs.

The elders attempted to quell the disquiet, but that task became increasingly difficult. They saw several families move on to other congregations. The more vocal remained, being viewed by the elders in various ways. Finally, in that morning's congregational meeting, a motion was made from the membership that the minister be dismissed. To the elders' dismay, a second was immediately given and the question called for and passed by a margin of 78%.

The results of their ignoring the issues and quelling the disquiet were obvious. The congregation had stagnated. It had fragmented itself into two groups: one (the majority) wanting the minister to leave, the other now feeling that a man had been grossly mistreated. A servant of God had come face to face with a reality that he could no longer deny and was deeply hurt. It would be several years before this congregation would recover.

With a positive view of conflict, opposing viewpoints can be expressed and shared without negative labels being attached; feelings of hurt and guilt can be resolved; and energy can be used for growth rather than for fighting. In such a climate, groups within congregations can continually move toward greater intimacy and wholeness because they learn to better handle the sharing of information and ideas. Even if the material under discussion is controversial, when a climate of acceptance is fostered without labels of sinfulness being attached, the effectiveness of the witness of that congregation will be increased. The attitude that is developed toward conflict will greatly affect the outcome of the conflict itself.

A young Navy lieutenant, a doctor, offered this comment about his congregation: "They are not afraid to tackle any topic. Nothing is off limits as far as discussion goes. Everyone is encouraged to speak his mind and to have input on any given issue. In contrast to other congregations that I have been a part of where one person or group spoke and everyone else fell into line, this congregation encourages you to share even if you disagree." His congregation is reaching a diverse group of individuals, military and civilian. These individuals have a variety of religious backgrounds or no background at all. Yet, through being encouraged constantly to share their beliefs and feelings, and being pointed to Scripture as the ultimate authority, they are being shaped into a viable, growing fellowship.

WHAT SHOULD BE DONE?

With such divergent views of conflict being espoused, it becomes necessary for every individual in leadership within the church to do two things. First of all, individuals must arrive at a biblical theology of conflict. Willimon states, "The pastor is not simply concerned that conflict in the church be managed, he is concerned that it be responded to in a way that is faithful, in a way that is congruent with the demands of the gospel."[9] Regardless of the seeming success of any method of conflict management, it must be placed under the authority of Scripture.

Second, persons in leadership positions must acquire skills in conflict management that are consistent with that theology. Willimon counsels, "The acquisition of skills in diagnosing the types and the dynamics of conflict is essential for effective pastoral response to church fights."[10] A fundamental skill is a self-awareness of how you deal with conflict situations. Leas says, "The way you are aware of yourself in conflict will profoundly affect your ability to manage yourself and work with others in the midst of a conflict."[11] From this point additional insights and skills can be acquired that will enable the leader to be effective in ministry.

In a recent survey given to forty-five ministers, associates, and others in church leadership positions within the Atlanta, Georgia, area, individuals were asked to give their response to ten statements relating to their involvement with conflict. They were asked to rate the statements on a scale of one to five, one being the lowest, five the highest.

In evaluating the responses to the questionnaire, several observations can be made. The items given the lowest ratings were predictable. Very little attention has been given in our colleges and seminaries to training individuals in the area of conflict management, resulting in a lack of knowledge of techniques and strategies. At any gathering of church leaders, conversations can be heard detailing the frustrations experienced over conflicts that have boiled up and overwhelmed the lives of congregations. Many times these frustrations center on the lack of knowledge of how to respond to the situation and bring it to resolution. There is a real need for training in the area.

One item that was given a mid-range rating was surprising. The perceived amount of conflict in churches was given a 3.4 rating. Based on conversations with church leaders and the number of conflict situations that arise in the life of any church, this rating would seem rather low.

The statements that were given the highest rating indicated the need and interest in training that would equip individuals to deal more adequately with conflict. This response was in direct proportion to the response given to those items dealing with previous training and the ability of church leaders to respond to conflict.

Conflict is a part of church life that must be faced from time to time by every normal congregation. Bob Russell in his book *Making Things Happen* says "disagreements are inevitable. Expect them."[12] Supporting this idea, McSwain and Treadwell assert, "Churches, like families and associates in work and play, experience conflict. Conflict is a facet of every human group."[13] This would seem to be true on the basis of observing congregational life today. Willimon goes so far as to say that "a church where there is a healthy amount of tension and conflict is a church alive."[14]

In fact, every leader within the church should expect to have to deal with some type of conflict if the congregation he serves is on the cutting edge of ministry. McSwain and Treadwell carry this idea one step further to assert that conflict is a necessary part of the church's existence.

> Is conflict necessary then? Yes, because sin has made its impression upon all persons. Must it be so prevalent in the church? Yes, for the church is a community of sinners being saved by grace. It has not yet been redeemed into God's future kingdom. Must I deal with conflict as a part of my commitment to his church? Yes, for any ministry of reconciliation assumes persons in need of reconciliation. If people refuse to recognize and deal with conflict, there can be no reconciliation.[15]

The leaders of God's church must be prepared to lead their people through and beyond these struggles, using each activity of ministry, including the preaching of the Word, to accomplish the task. Our preaching must address the needs of people to bring the Word to bear on each aspect of life, including conflict.

> For the preacher to attempt to remove his or her preaching from the conflict is to imply that the Bible is irrelevant for the church today and that preaching is too timid and detached to be of great help when the chips are down and we desperately need a guiding word.[16]

While this view may seem pessimistic to some, perhaps even non-biblical to others, it serves as the foundational idea for this book.

DEFINITION OF CONFLICT

Before we proceed any further, we must develop a working defi-nition of conflict if we are to understand what we are responding to and how to make that response. Perhaps a couple of definitions previously devised will give us some direction. Willimon defines conflict as "whenever two or more persons go after goals that they perceive to be mutually exclusive; whenever one person's needs collide with another's conflict results."[17] Jay Hall says that "conflict exists whenever there are important differences between people, groups, or nations which, should they persist and remain unre-solved, serve to keep the parties involved apart in some way."[18]

It is important to notice that neither of the above definitions deals with the aspect of behavior in the midst of conflict. It is vital that these two concepts be kept separate because conflict can exist without sinful behavior being involved as it does with John, a very capable, mature Christian who serves our congregation as an elder. He has a very high view of the Lord's Table and feels that commu-nion should be the focal point of worship for the believer. I totally agree with him in this and work to develop our worship experiences in light of this concept.

John, however, has carried this high view one step further by stating that he believes that the Lord's Table should be observed only during times of corporate worship. He and I have come into conflict over the Lord's Table being served at Christmas Eve services, youth retreats, and on other occasions. Even though the tone and atmosphere were definitely worshipful, it was not at a regular worship experience and in John's mind inappropriate.

Our debates on this issue have been private and admittedly forceful at times. They have, however, been conducted in the high-est language of respect and concern for the other person, but we have come to the conclusion that we disagree and will probably never agree about this particular point of opinion.

Where am I going with this? To this point: Conflict exists when two or more individuals approach a given issue from more than one perspective, resulting in apparent differences. There does not have to be sinful behavior (e.g., shouting matches, insults, or physical blows) for conflict to occur. In many cases the behavior which is feared and avoided at all costs comes when there is no resolution of the conflict. By resolution I do not necessarily mean agreement. John and I still disagree but there is respect for the other's opinion, as well as the understanding that the issue under discussion is not a vital one for our congregation.

Two Primary Views

As has been seen, two primary views of conflict exist within the church. The first equates conflict with sin and places high value on the avoidance of conflict. The second sees conflict as an inevitable and, yes, integral part of the church's growth. If the first is valid, this book should end here because the mere introduction of the subject can cause conflicts to erupt. If the second is more realistic and provides greater potential for the development of relationships and ministry within the church, then an initial attempt should be made to understand conflict from a biblical perspective. This attempt will be made in the next two chapters.

ENDNOTES

[1]Myron Rush, *Management: A Biblical Approach* (Wheaton, IL: Victor Books, 1987), p. 202.

[2]*Ibid.*, p. 203.

[3]Larry L. McSwain and William C. Treadwell, Jr., *Conflict Ministry in the Church.* (Nashville: Broadman, 1981), p. 117.

[4]William H. Willimon, *Preaching about Conflict in the Local Church* (Philadelphia: Westminster, 1987), p. 17.

[5]J. Robert Clinton, *The Making of a Leader.* (Colorado Springs: NavPress, 1988), p. 107.

[6]*Ibid.*, p. 163.

[7]McSwain and Treadwell, p. 35.

[8]Willimon, p. 44.

[9]*Ibid.*, p. 43.

[10]*Ibid.*, p. 14.

[11]Speed Leas, *Leadership and Conflict* (Nashville: Abingdon, 1982), p. 82.

[12]Bob Russell, *Making Things Happen* (Cincinnati: Standard, 1987), p. 69.

[13]McSwain and Treadwell, p. 29.

[14]Willimon, p. 15.

[15]McSwain and Treadwell, p. 24.

[16]Willimon, p. 9.

[17]*Ibid.*, p. 10.

[18]Jay Hill, *Conflict Management Survey* (The Woodlands: Teleometrics, 1986), p. 1.

CHAPTER 2

A THEOLOGY OF CONFLICT

As was pointed out in the previous chapter, one of the primary tasks of church leadership in managing conflict is the development of a theology of conflict management. Christians must determine the position to which Scripture commits them as methods of conflict management are developed. There are many conflict situations presented in Scripture as well as instructions for working through disagreements. To evaluate each situation exhaustively goes beyond the scope of this book. However, in order to begin such a theology, we will evaluate several passages of Scripture that deal with conflict in the relationship of God and his people, in the life and teachings of Jesus, and in the life of the first century church.

OLD TESTAMENT PASSAGES

Exodus 32:7-12

⁷Then the LORD said to Moses, "Go down, because your people, whom you brought up out of Egypt, have become corrupt. ⁸They have been quick to turn away from what I commanded them and have made themselves an idol cast in the shape of a calf. They have bowed down to it and sacrificed to it and have said, 'These are your gods, O Israel, who brought you up out of Egypt.' ⁹ "I have seen these people," the LORD said to Moses, "and they are a stiff-necked people. ¹⁰Now leave me alone so that my anger may burn against them and that I may destroy them. Then I will make you into a great nation." ¹¹But Moses sought the favor of the LORD his God. "O LORD," he said, "why should your anger

burn against your people, whom you brought out of Egypt with great power and a mighty hand? [12]Why should the Egyptians say, 'It was with evil intent that he brought them out, to kill them in the mountains and to wipe them off the face of the earth'? Turn from your fierce anger; relent and do not bring disaster on your people."

The setting of this passage is Mt. Sinai as God presented and made a covenant with his people. Moses on the mountain with God receives from the very hand of God the laws that would order his people. These laws would first designate them as a covenant people and would then provide a framework in which they would live and work together. Instruction had been given for the articles to be used in worship, each item being used functionally to remind them of the relationship they had covenanted with God. God provides Moses with stone tablets upon which his commandments have been written as Moses prepares to return and present them to the people.

However, as Moses was gone for an extended period of time, the people became restless. Perhaps their prolonged contact with Egyptian religion had solidified in their minds, bringing about the request for a concrete representation of the deity that had brought them out of Egypt. Perhaps their relationship with Moses was so fragile that his absence created doubt and fear in their hearts that could not be satisfied. In any event, their request for gods was honored by Aaron.

To further complicate the issue, Aaron proclaimed a day of sacrifice and festival. The fear of the Lord that had gripped their hearts as God descended upon Sinai disappeared and the moral restraints that Moses had placed upon them were ignored. It is in this context that Exodus 32:7-14 occurs.

Even though Moses is ignorant of the developments in the camp, God immediately makes him aware not only of the events themselves but also of the consequences of those events. In speaking of the people, God transfers ownership of them to Moses and the efforts of bringing them out of Egypt are credited to him as well.

God has cut himself off from these people in response to their pledge of allegiance to the calf of molten metal. God pronounces his judgment by directing Moses not to hinder him from destroying them for their sin. Going farther, he promises that from Moses he will develop a great nation.

In the face of this burst of God's righteous anger, Moses seeks to find favor with God. The connotation is one of appeasement as Moses endeavors to develop a compromise by offering two lines of argument. First, he asks what will be the view of God resulting in the minds of the Egyptians if (and notice that Moses denies responsibility and ownership) God has led Israel out into the mountains to be destroyed. Second, Moses encourages God to remember his promise to the patriarchs to make of them a great nation. On the basis of these two factors, God is encouraged by Moses to change his mind. At the presentation of these points of argument God does modify his position. The people, however, do feel the heavy hand of God as plague ravishes and they await his judgment.

God's Attitude Toward Conflict

In these events can be observed to some degree God's attitude toward conflict. In the face of the sin that Israel commits, God confronts Moses, declaring dire judgment on the people. God engages the conflict with great vigor. But when Moses dares to challenge God's reasoning with pointed arguments, God's anger is not redirected toward Moses as might be expected. He listens to the reasoning and alters his judgment.

In reality, this passage describes two different conflicts. The first is between God and the people, the second between Moses and God. The only sin that is present is in the disobedience of the people and it is labeled as such. No such label is attached to God's confrontation with Moses or the challenge to alter his judgment that Moses presents. The actions of the people are not without consequence as God and the people proceed in their covenant relationship.

Isaiah 1:18-20

[18]"Come now, let us reason together," says the LORD. "Though your sins are like scarlet, they shall be as white as snow; though they are red as crimson, they shall be like wool. —[19]If you are willing and obedient, you will eat the best from the land; [20]but if you resist and rebel, you will be devoured by the sword." For the mouth of the LORD has spoken.

In the verses of the opening chapter of the book of Isaiah, God states his case against Judah and Jerusalem. He has raised them and they have rebelled (Isaiah 1:2). They are a sinful people, having forsaken the Lord and having spurned the Holy One of Israel (Isaiah 1:4-5). He points out that they have been wounded and afflicted and their cities have been wasted. Even though they have offered multitudes of sacrifices, they have forgotten the concepts of right, justice, and the causes of the oppressed and fatherless (Isaiah 1:11, 17).

It is in the context of Judah's disobedience that God issues his proposal. "Come now" is a phrase that conveys various emotions and is used by individuals of different positions: an equal to an equal, a superior to an inferior, and an inferior to a superior.

It is normally the introductory remark for a proposal that has mutual benefit for all parties involved or at least benefit for the party being addressed. God, in spite of Judah's sin, still has their best interests at heart.

The proposal is an invitation for Judah to come and discuss their relationship with God. The word that is translated "reason together" is used in other passages to denote the giving of judicial decisions and in situations where the imagery of a law court or judgment is introduced. Examples of this type of imagery can be found in Job 13:3, Psalm 50:8, and Proverbs 24:25. Even though this is a possible interpretation, another possibility may exist. The word may also mean to reprove one another, to point out one another's faults, to discuss with one another who is right and who is wrong. God is inviting Judah to discuss the nature of their relationship to determine what is the appropriate course of action. From the context it is obvious the outcome of such a discussion, but still God invites Judah to discuss the issues.

The offer that God presents to Judah is one of forgiveness. Even though in response to their moral conduct Judah may be in line for the retributive justice of God, he presents them the opportunity to benefit from his compassion and mercy. Not only will he forgive sins that are scarlet and crimson, they will be as wool and snow.

These statements of forgiveness precede two conditional statements that point out the consequences of their ongoing actions. These statements present two alternatives. Acceptance of and obedience to God's moral standards will result in their eating the good of the land. Refusal and rebellion hold their being consumed by the sword.

God's Confrontation of the Conflict

Obviously a conflict exists between God and Judah and is the result of Judah's sin. Rather than ignore the conflict, God confronts the differences that exist between Judah's behavior and his standards. His invitation to examine the differences and his offer of forgiveness present an opportunity to arrive at a solution that will benefit the people and uphold his righteousness. It is unfortunate that with the exception of a few individuals, this collaborative attempt on God's part was ignored by the nation as a whole.

The attitude that God expresses here is closely related to that expressed in the previous passage studied. Sinful behavior is labeled as such, but God enters the conflict, issuing an invitation to Judah to discuss the issues. His offering of forgiveness further underlines his willingness to work with these people in spite of their previous actions.

SUMMARY

If God's actions are to serve as a model for leadership within his church, then these Old Testament passages offer these suggestions. One, the presence of conflict does not necessarily denote sin; e.g., Moses' disagreement with God. Two, sin can be present in conflict as in the behavior patterns of Israel. Three, conflict must be engaged if a positive solution is to be derived. This God does in both passages. Finally, suggestions must be offered that will benefit all individuals. This is especially true of God's actions in the second passage.

In order to gain further insight into the biblical concept of conflict, we must now turn our attention to the life and teachings of Jesus.

CHAPTER 3

NEW TESTAMENT PASSAGES

Mark 11:15-17

¹⁵On reaching Jerusalem, Jesus entered the temple area and began driving out those who were buying and selling there. He overturned the tables of the money changers and the benches of those selling doves, ¹⁶and would not allow anyone to carry merchandise through the temple courts. ¹⁷And as he taught them, he said, "Is it not written: 'My house will be called a house of prayer for all nations'? But you have made it 'a den of robbers.'"

This particular event in the life of Jesus occurs at the beginning of his final week of ministry, the day after his entry into Jerusalem when the crowds proclaimed him King. As most of the events of that week, this particular episode gave increasing validation to his claim of being the Messiah. Malachi 3:1-3 points to the day that the Lord himself would enter the temple and with the refiner's fire would purify the worship of Israel. It is in the area of worship that Jesus focuses his attention, fulfilling the prophecy of Malachi.

Upon entering Jerusalem, Jesus entered the temple area. Especially for individuals that would travel to Jerusalem from distant places, provision had to be made within the context of the temple itself for items needed to fulfill the obligations of the sacrificial system. The scene that greeted the eyes of Jesus was one of unbridled commerce rather than simply meeting the needs of pilgrims. It was at this point that Jesus cast out the sellers, buyers, and moneychangers.

If the picture that we have of Jesus is one of total calm and serenity, then this and other parallel passages completely destroy this image. Jesus was upset and his anger was translated into the use of force as he overturned tables and drove out those who were engaged in profit making.

Following the expulsion of the buyers and sellers, Jesus takes the opportunity to teach and express to the disciples the rationale behind his actions. He quotes from two passages: Isaiah 56:7 and Jeremiah 7:11. Isaiah 56 records God promising that his blessings will be shared with all people. Mark records the entire verse of Isaiah 56:7, emphasizing that the nations were to share in this proclamation. The second passage that Jesus quotes, Jeremiah 7:11, declares that the authorities have made the temple a den of robbers. Jeremiah had warned Judah of the folly of standing before God within the temple while at the same time committing such sins as murder, perjury, and the worship of idols (Jeremiah 7:9-10). Jesus proclaims final fulfillment of this passage in his day.

Even though much could be said of the dishonest practices used by the merchandisers within the confines of the temple, the real theft that was occurring was a spiritual one. Because of the commerce based in the Court of the Gentiles within the temple area, the Jews were robbing the Gentiles of their rightful ability to worship God. This was the real issue which motivated the actions of Jesus.

Jesus' Response to Problems

This is one of the most extreme examples of the manner in which Jesus dealt with problems. Jesus, like his Heavenly Father, is quick to enter conflict even to the extreme of using forceful actions to convey his point. He does not shrink from or avoid the issue but tackles it head on. This method of directly dealing with an issue is not an isolated tactic; cf. his confrontation with the Pharisees, Matthew 23; his dealing with faithless disciples, Matthew 17:14-21; and his relationships with individuals struggling with sin, Luke 19:1-10.

A case could and should be made that leaders within the church today do not have the same range of authority as Jesus exercised. Obviously the application of righteous anger, such as Jesus had at the desecration of his Father's house, should be tempered with proper behavior. However, the lack of timidity when dealing with problems, sorting them out, and bringing them to a satisfactory conclusion should be emulated. In the next passages under consideration Jesus gives his prescription for how this should be done.

Matthew 5:23-24

23 "Therefore, if you are offering your gift at the altar and there remember that your brother has something against you, 24leave your gift there in front of the altar. First go and be reconciled to your brother; then come and offer your gift."

Matthew 18:15-17

15 "If your brother sins against you, go and show him his fault, just between the two of you. If he listens to you, you have won your brother over. 16But if he will not listen, take one or two others along, so that 'every matter may be established by the testimony of two or three witnesses.' 17If he refuses to listen to them, tell it to the church; and if he refuses to listen even to the church, treat him as you would a pagan or a tax collector."

The first of these passages occurs in the midst of the Sermon on the Mount. The immediate context deals with the seriousness and consequences of unrighteous anger. This passage is placed in the setting of worship and stresses that unresolved anger does affect the way that we worship.

Jesus begins the section in verse 21 by addressing the total group of listeners, but with verse 23 changes the focus of his teaching to the individual. Jesus in doing this makes this lesson very personal. He does not mention the personal anger that an individual might experience in such an exchange, but rather deals with the offense you have caused. Carson remarks, "We are more likely to remember when we have something against others than when we have done something to offend others. And if we are truly concerned about our anger and hate, we will be no less concerned when we engender them in others."[1]

In this passage Jesus places the responsibility for reconciling a conflict in the hands of the one who has caused the problem. The individual is not to avoid the issue, because to do so invalidates the gift that is being presented. He is to initiate the process of reconciliation, and when it has been accomplished, then return and engage in formal worship.

The second passage occurs in the midst of a discourse that has the concept of forgiveness as one of its themes. In the opening verses of the chapter, the disciples raise the question as to who is the greatest in the kingdom of heaven. (Cf. Mark 9:33-38 and Luke 9:46-48.) It is apparent that there is rivalry among the disciples, which prompts the question. There follow in Matthew teachings concerning humility (vv. 3-4), the problem of causing another to sin and the removal of that cause (vv. 5-9), the parable of the shepherd who seeks the one lost sheep (vv. 10-14), and, following the passage under discussion, Jesus' response to Peter's question concerning the quantity of forgiveness and the parable of the unmerciful servant. Within this context Jesus in these verses offers to the disciples a method for dealing with offenses and the resolution of the conflict they produce.

Jesus' Method for Resolving Conflict

The presence or absence of the phrase "against you" provides two possible interpretations for these verses.[2] If "against you" is omitted, then Jesus is providing general instruction for the community as to how to handle a sinful brother. If the prepositional phrase is to be included, Jesus is looking at the offenses from the viewpoint of the brother against whom the offense is committed.

In either case the guidance given by Jesus is to confront the individual privately and express the feelings prompted by the brother's actions. This concept is further supported in Galatians 6:1 where Paul encourages the brothers, "Even if a man is caught in any trespass, you who are spiritual, restore such a one in a spirit of gentleness; looking to yourself, lest you too be tempted."

As Christians we are commanded by Scripture to deal with issues as they arise in order to bring about the restoration of relationships and to lovingly dissuade those who are traveling paths toward spiritual ruin. It is a call for involvement in the lives of other believers.

Carol called and asked for an appointment. Upon meeting her at the office, she very tearfully shared the reason for her distress: I was it. Her brother's child had become critically ill, and because of my involvement in a youth activity lasting the entire day and later simply because of exhaustion, I did not respond to that need until the next day. She was very hurt and very angry because of my apparent lack of sensitivity.

My response was a simple one: "I'm sorry." Not only was she correct in feeling that I should have responded in a more timely fashion, but she was also correct in the way that she handled her feelings. She carried out the teaching of Christ.

The word "reprove" has as its primary meaning to bring to light, expose, or set forth. In this context it carries the connotation of refuting. The purpose of this reproof is not to win points but to prompt the brother's hearing of the issue with the result of your winning over your brother. Carson states, "All discipline, even this private kind, must begin with redemptive purposes."[3]

Jesus goes on to point out (verse 16) that the possibility exists that the individual will not listen to what is being said.

The offended individual upon this lack of hearing is enjoined to take one or two more. The purpose is that through the testimony of two or three witnesses, the truth may be established or made to stand.

This second step is not without precedent. Deuteronomy 19:15 requires that before the conviction of an individual there must be two or three witnesses who present their evidence. This same principle is followed by Paul (1 Timothy 5:19) in his instructions to Timothy concerning accusations made against an elder.

The inclusion of witnesses in this procedure could serve two purposes. If these individuals had witnessed the event under discussion, their awareness of the facts would give extra weight to the one confronting the wayward brother. They would be able to give testimony concerning this discussion if the matter was not resolved and had to be taken before the assembly. In either case the purpose is still redemptive. Their purpose is not to threaten or to intimidate the brother into repentance but to add emphasis to the seriousness of the situation.

If the individual refuses to listen to this group, a further step is encouraged. In this case, refusal to listen to the group that is attempting to deal with the problem results in the matter being told to the church. At this particular time the church as such was not in existence, and so the idea being conveyed is that the matter is to be shared with the congregation, the assembly of believers. A refusal to listen to the assembly results in the offender being dealt with as a Gentile and tax collector. The individual simply is to be put out of the fellowship, excommunicated. Even though this is an extreme measure, its purpose is still restorative in nature, motivated by love and concern for the spiritual welfare of the individual.

Summary

In both of the above passages, Jesus provides instruction for dealing with interpersonal conflict. Whether the individual is causing or receiving the offense is irrelevant. In either event the disciple is to initiate the process of reconciliation by going to the opposing individual. It is desired that this step in the process will facilitate a solution to the issue. If not, Jesus adds a second, third, and, if needed, fourth step.

The second step involves the incorporation of others to aid in the sorting out of details, the determination of the truth of matters, and the arbitration of solutions. In the event that this is fruitless, the third step of telling the matter to the church must be taken. The church becomes the final court of appeal. If the offender refuses the church's counsel, he is to be dealt with as one outside the family with the same love and concern any non- believer is shown.

Obviously, not all interpersonal conflicts would require that all of the above-mentioned steps be implemented. Only in those instances where clearly sinful behavior has been involved should the total procedure be carried out. Nevertheless, the model presented by Jesus encourages believers not to overlook differences but to deal with them, involving others where needed, to arrive at conclusions that maintain relationships and uphold God's standards of behavior.

Acts 6:1-6

[1]In those days when the number of disciples was increasing, the Grecian Jews among them complained against the Hebraic Jews because their widows were being overlooked in the daily distribution of food. [2]So the Twelve gathered all the disciples together and said, "It would not be right for us to neglect the ministry of the word of God in order to wait on tables. [3]Brothers, choose seven men from among you who are known to be full of the Spirit and wisdom. We will turn this responsibility over to them [4]and will give our attention to prayer and the ministry of the word." [5]This proposal pleased the whole group. They chose Stephen, a man full of faith and of the Holy Spirit; also Philip, Procorus, Nicanor, Timon, Parmenas, and Nicolas from Antioch, a convert to Judaism. [6]They presented these men to the apostles, who prayed and laid their hands on them.

Growth Sometimes Brings Problems

These verses record further progression in the development of the early church. The church had come into existence on Pentecost and experienced rapid growth from its inception. Luke records an initial three thousand converts whose number had grown to over five thousand (Acts 2:41; 4:4). The church had experienced rapid spiritual growth as well. Individuals continually shared their wealth to meet the needs of others. The church had survived the initial persecution brought on by the preaching of the gospel and the internal problems created by Ananias and Sapphira. The progress was undeniable.

It is in this context that a murmuring arose. The parties that were involved in this disagreement are identified by Luke as Hellenists and Hebrews. The differences between these groups may have only been in language (Greek versus Hebrew) or geographic location (those born in Palestine over against those born in foreign countries). A more significant dissimilarity may have been in their mental orientation, the Hebrews maintaining a more orthodox approach to the observance of the law and Jewish customs versus those who had adopted a Greek lifestyle and worldview.

The situation that prompted the murmuring was a substantial one. The Hellenistic widows were overlooked in the daily distribution of food. Luke indicates that the neglect was not just a momentary lapse but that it had gone on for some time. Whether this was deliberate neglect brought about by ethnic prejudice or some other unrecorded motivation or was a matter of simple oversight is not mentioned. As situations left untended often do, this one resulted in a clash between groups.

Responsiveness of Leadership

The response of the Twelve was to call together the multitude of the disciples. Up to this point the leadership of the assembly rested in the hands of the apostles. Rather than ignoring or avoiding the issue, they very quickly and wisely decided to deal with the short-lived discomfort of responding to the complaint.

Their remarks point to an understanding of ministry that allowed for differences in gifts and functions among people. The Twelve understood that they had been called to a particular ministry, the word of God. To leave that ministry to serve tables would not be pleasing. They recognized that priorities needed to be established, with this priority being better handled by others.

The Twelve suggest an alternative, the selection of seven men that would be appointed over this office. In suggesting this alterna-tive, the Twelve were in no way demeaning the ministry or those whose needs were targeted by it. This would allow the apostles to continue in the areas of preaching, teaching, and leading in worship with others being given the freedom and responsibility of seeing that this need was met.

Three basic qualities were to adhere to the men who were to be chosen. They were first of all to be men attested to by the disciples. They were to be men whose lives had been observed to be of good character. Second, they were to be full of the Spirit, their spiritual maturity was to be evident. Finally, they were to possess wisdom. These characteristics may seem rather strong for such a simple task as food distribution. But was it so simple?

The situation was a precarious one. Individuals had divided themselves into two opposing groups. Murmuring had begun. The need was for men whose integrity was above question. This task involving physical things was of a highly spiritual nature involving the well-being of an unprotected group. God's Spirit would certainly be needed to meet not only the physical needs but also any other that was found. These men must possess in real measure the ability to wisely decide on the ministry's administration. Hurts needed heal-ing, and wisdom would be required to do this effectively and effi-ciently.

The disciples viewed this suggestion with pleasure. (Note the use of pleasing in this context, as well as in verse two when used to describe the Twelve leaving the ministry of the word. Proper solutions produce pleasure.) Seven men were chosen.

Each of the names listed is Greek in form. One might assume that since the Hellenists were the offended party, they were the ones given the responsibility of rectifying it. This may be true, but it may also be that individuals of both parties possessed Greek names or the Greek equivalent of their Hebrew name.

The results of this resolution were dramatic. The word of God grew. The form of the Greek verb denotes a continuous action. The word is used to describe the growth of plants and children. (See Luke 13:19 and Luke 2:40.) It was a qualitative increase that also bore fruit in the multiplication of the disciples which included a large number of priests.

Principles Involved in Conflict Resolution

In this passage, which records one of the first intergroup conflicts within the church, several principles of conflict management can be derived. First of all, groups involved in conflict should not necessarily be labeled as sinful. Luke does not attach blame or find fault as he records the event. Second, differences are best handled when brought out into the open and discussed. In calling the meeting and discussing the issue forthrightly, the apostles diffused a potentially dangerous situation that avoidance, with its attendant murmuring, would only have made more critical. Third, these men suggested an alternative that was agreeable to both groups. Each group perceived themselves to be winners as a result of the decision. Finally, rather than disastrous results, the church continued to experience dramatic growth. The church, having resolved a potentially crippling issue, could direct its energies toward sharing the word while continuing to meet the needs of its constituency.

Acts 15:1-21

[1]Some men came down from Judea to Antioch and were teaching the brothers: "Unless you are circumcised, according to the custom taught by Moses, you cannot be saved." [2]This brought Paul and Barnabas into sharp dispute and debate with them. So Paul and Barnabas were appointed, along with some other believers, to go up to Jerusalem to see the apostles and elders about this question. [3]The church sent them on their way, and as they traveled through Phoenicia and Samaria, they told how the Gentiles had been converted. This news made all the brothers very glad. [4]When they came to Jerusalem, they were welcomed by the church and the apostles and elders, to whom they reported everything God had done through them. [5]Then some of the believers who belonged to the party of the Pharisees stood up and said, "The Gentiles must be circumcised and required to obey the law of Moses." [6]The apostles and elders met to consider this question. [7]After much discussion, Peter got up and addressed them: "Brothers, you know that some time ago God made a choice among you that the Gentiles might hear from my lips the message of the gospel and believe. [8]God, who knows the heart, showed that he accepted them by giving the Holy Spirit to them, just as he did to us. [9]He made no distinction between us and them, for he purified their hearts by faith. [10]Now then, why do you try to test God by putting on the necks of the disciples a yoke that neither we nor our fathers have been able to bear? [11]No! We believe it is through the grace of our Lord Jesus that we are saved, just as they are." [12]The whole assembly became silent as they listened to Barnabas and Paul telling about the miraculous signs and wonders God had done among the Gentiles through them. [13]When they finished, James spoke up: "Brothers, listen to me. [14]Simon has described to us how God at first showed his concern by taking from the Gentiles a people for himself. [15]The words of the prophets are in agreement with this, as it is written: [16]'After this I will return and rebuild David's fallen tent. Its ruins I will rebuild, and I will restore it, [17]that the remnant of men may seek the Lord, and all

the Gentiles who bear my name, says the Lord, who does these things' [18]that have been known for ages. [19]It is my judgment, therefore, that we should not make it difficult for the Gentiles who are turning to God. [20]Instead we should write to them, telling them to abstain from food polluted by idols, from sexual immorality, from the meat of strangled animals and from blood. [21]For Moses has been preached in every city from the earliest times and is read in the synagogues on every Sabbath."

The events of Acts 15 follow Luke's account of Paul's and Barnabas' first missionary tour and their subsequent report of those events to the church in Antioch. Many individuals had responded to the gospel as a result of their preaching, many from among the Gentiles.

It is to the church at Antioch that individuals from Judea came down, teaching that unless they were circumcised by the custom of Moses, they could not be saved. The occasion for this mission to Antioch is unknown. Perhaps the most simple answer is that it was the first congregation where Jews and Gentiles came together to form a single fellowship of believers. Those that came should probably be identified with the sect of believing Pharisees found in verse five.

The addition of the act of circumcision to the gospel message was no small matter. In essence they were asserting that the road to Christ passed first through the Mosaic law, to become a Christian involved first becoming a Jew. This was not a small issue; either salvation was based in the grace of Jesus Christ or it was rooted in a system of merit and works. The entire nature of Christianity is affected by which position is adopted.

Luke says that as a result of this teaching Paul and Barnabas engaged in "discord" and "not a little questioning." The combination of the two words underlines the serious nature of the discussions. These debates were heated exchanges where values were at stake, values that centered around the nature of the gospel.

As a result of these ongoing debates, with little resolution occurring, the church at Antioch sent Paul, Barnabas, and some of the others to meet with the apostles and elders at Jerusalem. En route to Jerusalem through Phoenicia and Samaria, they told in detail of the conversion of the Gentiles, bringing joy to the brethren. Because the brothers were converted from the Hellenists' preaching following the killing of Stephen, there was in all probability a broader view present among the Phoenicians and Samaritans than was evidenced in Jerusalem, resulting in the news of the Gentile conversion being received with joy. This report continued upon their arrival at Jerusalem as the apostles, elders, and the church welcomed them.

In contrast to their message, the Pharisaic sect stated their position beginning with the word "it is necessary." With the use of the Greek word from which the phrase "it is necessary" is translated, the Pharisaic sect is implying that the issue is not just a matter of expedience but of the revealed will of God.

This brought about another round of debate, conducted no doubt with the same intensity and heat as the debates in Antioch.

Responding to the debate, Peter rises and is given the opportunity to speak. In referring to Peter's remarks Bruce says, "He reminded the company that the fundamental principle which they were discussing had already been decided, when nearly ten years before he had been led to the house of Cornelius and Gentiles had heard the gospel for the first time from his lips."[4] He questions their testing God by placing the yoke of the law on the neck of the disciples. Bruce, in commenting on Peter and the others, says, "They recognized that their own salvation was due to the free grace of Christ; were they to acknowledge another principle of salvation for Gentile believers?"[5]

Following Peter's presentation, the crowd was silent and listened to the account of Paul and Barnabas. They rehearsed the signs and wonders that God did through them. Theirs was not a report of self-aggrandizement but of praise to God for his mighty acts, implying that God had put his stamp of approval on their ministry through the vehicle of miracles and signs.

After the report of Barnabas and Paul, James calls the assembly to order with the formal address, "men and brothers," requesting their attention. In discussing the leadership qualities of James the Lord's brother, it must be noted that while being very rigorous in his own practice of the faith, he was more broad-minded than many who would have thought him their champion. His remarks effectively sum up the emerging view of the group.

James leaves the report of Paul and Barnabas out of his remarks, according to Luke's account. It may be that Luke is simply giving a condensation of the speech, as is entirely possible; but it may be an intentional strategy that James employs to carry his audience.

James, in referring to Simon's remarks, expressed his feelings clearly on the issue at hand. By calling the Gentile believers a people whom God had taken for his name, James did two things:

(1) he applied to Gentile Christians a designation heretofore used exclusively for Israel, and

(2) he agreed with Peter that God had initially inaugurated a direct Gentile ministry without the trappings of Judaism. James effectively shifted the Gentiles from a status of being proselytes to being integrally involved in their own right in the plan of God. He accomplishes this shift in his use of Amos 9:11-12.

This quotation is both textually and exegetically difficult. In linking the restoration of the Davidic house with the incorporation of the Gentiles, James is saying that the Gentile mission is not to be confused with the efforts of proselytizing but is an integral part of God's plan of reconciliation through Jesus Christ. Salvation and incorporation into the church were to be on the same basis, the free gift of God's grace.

James then turns to the practical considerations of how this incorporation must be lived out. These considerations would be presented in written form so that there would be no misinterpretation. Two types of issues were involved in this meeting. The first was a theological question dealing with the relationship of the necessity of circumcision and adherence to Jewish law with salvation. The assembly rejected the idea that there was any relationship. The four points suggested by James deal with the second consideration of how Gentiles would live with their Jewish brothers without causing offense and further difficulties. Since Moses is proclaimed and read in every city, the scruples of the Jewish brothers are to be respected.

How Was the Conflict Handled?

This passage provides several key insights with respect to the management of conflict. First of all, the issues were brought out into the open and discussed in great detail. They were not ignored under the pretense that they would go away. Many times issues that are swept under the carpet or put back into closets have a tendency to grow even larger while, at least on the surface, being ignored.

Second, when there was little hope for resolution, the church at Antioch sent individuals to Jerusalem for help in coming to grips with and resolving the issue. There is nothing wrong with asking for help, especially when the issue at stake involves the values that individuals would be willing to die for. It is unfortunate that many of us who are Christians in independent churches have stressed our independence to the extent that we have not availed ourselves of the help that at times is available from a third party, especially help that would enable us to resolve many of the conflicts that our congregations face.

Third, in the meetings in Jerusalem each party was given ample opportunity to state its case. No one could claim that he was slighted.

Fourth, Scripture was allowed to speak. Not only were the writings of Amos given a hearing, but also the way that God had acted previously. God's will revealed in his actions with the household of Cornelius was applied to all of the Gentiles.

Finally, the solution that was offered dealt with all the issues involved, both theological and practical. This solution was communicated in written form and ultimately attested to by other individuals so there would be no confusion.

Acts 15:36-41

[36]Some time later Paul said to Barnabas, "Let us go back and visit the brothers in all the towns where we preached the word of the Lord and see how they are doing." [37]Barnabas wanted to take John, also called Mark, with them, [38]but Paul did not think it wise to take him, because he had deserted them in Pamphylia and had not continued with them in the work. [39]They had such a sharp disagreement that they parted company. Barnabas took Mark and sailed for Cyprus, [40]but Paul chose Silas and left, commended by the brothers to the grace of the Lord. [41]He went through Syria and Cilicia, strengthening the churches.

In the first part of Acts 15, the church survived a major conflict between two opposing groups of believers. The schism that had threatened the entire body of Christ dealing with the grounds of salvation had not materialized. Issues had been resolved and the means of communicating that resolution had been settled. Paul, Barnabas, and those sent from Jerusalem had returned to Antioch where they and their message were warmly received. Paul and Barnabas remained in Antioch for some time continuing their program of teaching and preaching.

After some days, Paul made a suggestion to Barnabas that a return visit be made to the churches established on their first tour. To this suggestion Barnabas appeared to agree, adding that he wished to take with them John Mark.

Paul's response to Barnabas' suggestion was negative. Luke notes that his insistence was ongoing that Mark should not go, that he did not want Mark along on a day-to-day basis. Paul, apparently for reasons stemming from Mark's initial unreliability, took an adamant position about any future association. Paul could not forget that Mark had deserted them in Pamphylia. The reason behind his desertion is not given; perhaps it was homesickness or disagreement over Paul's Gentile policy.

This disagreement was not easily resolved; in fact, it resulted in sharp feelings that led to the separation of Paul from Barnabas. The end result was two, rather than one, missionary teams on the field, Paul taking Silas to Syria and Cilicia, and Barnabas taking Mark to Cyprus.

In this personal disagreement each man had valid points of concern, Paul for the strength and effectiveness of the team and Barnabas for the ongoing growth of Mark. One could argue either case. Even when individuals share the same basic concepts of faith, differences in perceptions, ideas, and experiences many times will lead two individuals to differing conclusions. Christians should learn that, in conflict, opposing views can have validity and that godly men may possess different views.

The solution was an agreement that disagreement existed and that each must go his separate way. It would seem that Scripture recognizes that this will occur and that God uses this at times to further his purpose. A change in attitude seems to be apparent from Paul's later writings. (See 1 Corinthians 9:6, Colossians 4:10, 2 Timothy 4:11, Philemon 24.) This separation gave Paul the opportunity to observe from afar and to alter his views while continuing to carry out his ministry.

SUMMARY

It is a primary concern that any concept of management which is used by leadership within the church has its base on firm theological footing. The study of these situations in which conflict has occurred offers such a base.

First of all, God is involved in conflict. In the Sinai experience and in the presence of his son Jesus as he clears the temple, God confronts those with whom he is in conflict. Even when Moses disagrees with God's decision to eliminate Israel and begin a new line with Moses, God remains in the discussion and ultimately modifies his decision.

In each of these situations, the actual process of conflict that is recorded is not labeled as sinful; neither are the individuals labeled as sinful because of the conflict. It is true that there can be sinful behavior in the midst of conflict, as seen in the worship of the calf idol and the perversion of worship in the temple. The Bible, however, is very clear in its separation of the two ideas. One is labeled sin while the other is not. Therefore, when confronted with conflict, leaders should not hurriedly look for the presence of sin as the rationale for conflict.

Equally true, Scripture is very quick to condemn division, dissension, and a party spirit. (See 1 Corinthians 3, Galatians 5.) These seem, however, to be the results of unresolved conflict rather than being a by-product of all conflict. In fact, the opposite situation of growth, greater maturity, and expanded ministry occurs in those situations where conflict is handled properly, as in Acts 6 and 15. The potential for enhanced growth is present in every conflict, even where sinful behavior is apparent.

Second, there are different types of conflict with differing catalysts present in Scripture. There is individual-group conflict where an individual stands against an entire body; interpersonal conflict involving two individuals; and intergroup conflict with groups of individuals differing. The catalysts are just as varied. Conflict may center around values (e.g., salvation requiring circumcision); goals (e.g., all widows being cared for); or methods (e.g., John Mark going on the next tour). This should prompt leadership of the church today to make a careful evaluation of any present conflict situation to determine the exact nature of the problem being confronted.

Finally, the Bible presents several methods for dealing with conflict. For interpersonal conflict, Jesus prescribes first of all a private meeting between the parties. Others are then involved if this initial discussion proves fruitless. Finally, if this does not resolve the issue, the entire church is to be involved with discipline of extreme forms used if the church is not heard.

The objection can be raised that Paul and Barnabas did not follow this procedure. However, a form of resolution did occur as they parted company and went separate ways. Luke does not record further backbiting or outbursts of anger that would indicate dissatisfaction with the situation. In fact, other passages point to an ultimate resolution of the situation in Paul's writings.

In Acts 6 and 15, procedures for handling intergroup conflict can be determined. First of all, there is clear and open discussion concerning the issues involved. Everyone is given opportunity to state his position. Second, outside help is sought, especially seen in Acts 15, when resolution is not forthcoming. Third, Scripture and the evident actions of God are brought to bear on the situation. As the groups move closer toward resolution, suggestions are made that allow each group to obtain what they need to maintain unity of purpose and ministry. Finally, the groups move beyond the issue to renewed growth and witness in the context of celebration.

When collected together, these concepts should enable leaders within today's church to evaluate the theories and methods of conflict management currently in use. Any method that ignores the value of individuals and their needs and ideas should be rejected. This should also be true for those procedures that remove individual responsibility for conflict resolution or attempt to label conflict as a negative force to be avoided at all costs.

ENDNOTES

[1]D.A. Carson, *Matthew* (Grand Rapids: Zondervan, 1984), p. 150.

[2]For a more complete discussion of this textual variant, see Carson, p. 404. For textual support for each option see the *Greek New Testament* (New York: United Bible Society, 1966), p. 69.

[3]Carson, p. 402.

[4]F.F. Bruce, *Commentary on the Book of Acts* (Grand Rapids: Eerdmans, 1968), p. 306.

[5]*Ibid.,* p. 307.

CHAPTER 4
THE NATURE OF CONFLICT

What is conflict? On the surface this seems to be a fairly simple question which should have an equally simple answer, but this is not the case. Willimon defines conflict as "whenever two or more persons go after goals that they perceive to be mutually exclusive; whenever one person's needs collide with another's conflict results."[1] Jay Hall's definition states that "conflict exists whenever there are important differences between people, groups, or nations which, should they persist and remain unresolved, serve to keep the parties involved apart in some way."[2]

In the first definition, conflict is presented as involving more than one person and is expanded in the second to include not only individuals but also groups and possibly nations. Willimon also points out that the basis of conflict may be in the pursuit of different goals or in the satisfaction of perceived needs. Jay Hall points out that conflict can result in barriers being erected that can separate individuals from one another, possibly on a permanent basis.

Conflict, then, is a very complex reality. It touches every individual, group, or congregation at some time. To begin to understand the nature of conflict is to accept the idea that conflict can be more than just a difference in personalities. Issues may be involved that have far-reaching implications for the individuals caught up in conflict. Attention must be given to these issues to determine what type of conflict is being experienced if there is to be any hope of resolving the conflict.

PLANES OF CONFLICT

Intrapersonal Plane

Conflict can be experienced on any or all of three different levels (see illustration, opposite). The first level is the intrapersonal plane. These conflicts occur within an individual, resulting from a variety of circumstances. There may be a lack or loss of self-esteem, a constant sense of failure regardless of achievements, or internalized anger that is never faced or resolved. Conflicts on this plane are best dealt with through individual counseling, therapy, study, or other methods that are directed toward personal change. If conflicts on this level are not resolved, the individual may well face conflicts on the second plane.

John was a young, very talented man who sat across the room, tearfully telling me the story of the breakup of his marriage. Prior to their marriage he and his wife had done all the right things. They had dated extensively and sought premarital counseling, and when those sessions raised some concerns they had attempted to work through them.

Immediately after their wedding, however, things began to go awry. His wife Joan began to distance herself from him emotionally and physically. This process culminated after three years when she refused to relocate with him following a new job assignment. Seeking further help, Joan finally revealed to their counselor that she had been molested as a child and raped during her late teen years. The intrapersonal conflict that these events caused had been suppressed for many years, only to come forward in her mind following their marriage.

Interpersonal Plane

Interpersonal conflicts exist on the second level of conflict. These conflicts deal with that form of conflict that occurs between

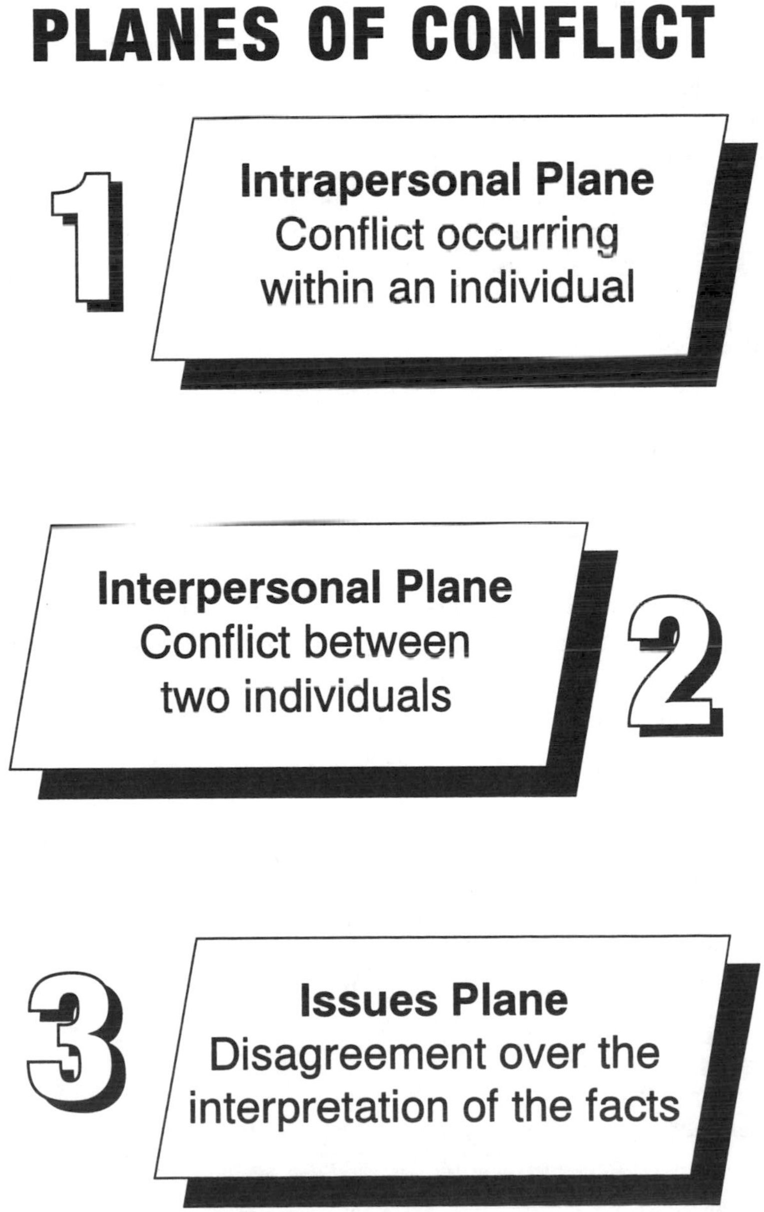

PLANES OF CONFLICT

1

Intrapersonal Plane
Conflict occurring
within an individual

Interpersonal Plane
Conflict between
two individuals

2

3

Issues Plane
Disagreement over the
interpretation of the facts

Figure 1.

two individuals. This form does not deal with issues per se but with differences in people. Each of us has been involved with others where our personality and theirs did not click. These conflicts for the most part are rather superficial, but differences between individuals can take on serious consequences within a marriage, business partnership (remember George and John and their involvement in the lumber business), or church staff relationships.

Ralph, the senior minister, a man in his early sixties, was having a very difficult time with Tom, a part-time staff member working with the youth of the congregation. He viewed Tom as a credible worker but one who needed to be more sensitive to the effects of change and more thorough in his preparation and planning. Tom, still a student at the nearby Bible college, was full of energy, enthusiastic about his work, and somewhat impatient at the conservative, possibly negative approach that he perceived Ralph adopted about every idea or program that Tom presented.

Through the efforts of a perceptive elder, Ralph and Tom were invited to share their feelings and work through the differences in perception that were present before any serious breakdown in their relationship could occur. Therapy and counseling (e.g., marriage and staff counseling) are ways in which these interpersonal forms of conflict can be dealt with effectively.

Issues Plane

The third plane of conflict deals with conflict of a substantive nature that arises out of issues. These issues are of four types: facts, means, ends, or values. Factual conflict may be a disagreement over facts or the interpretation of facts.

Mike was the third minister of a suburban congregation that had a ten-year history. The first minister had been an aggressive church planter who had worked for three years to see the congregation established. The second had served the congregation for six years, taking the congregation through an initial building program and establishing several long-term expressions of ministry. Now, at the end of his first year of service, Mike faces a conflict with the leadership of the congregation.

In a recent meeting of the leadership, two of the elders had voiced concerns over what they perceived as a negative rate of growth. Even though not specifically critical of Mike's work, their comments were interpreted by him as criticism of his ministry.

Mike was at a crucial point in ministry. He very well could react negatively to the concerns that had been stated by becoming defensive or antagonistic toward the elders, which could ultimately lead to a total breakdown in relationships. On the other hand, he could take a positive view of the conflict by hearing the concerns of the elders, spending some time in evaluating the past and present growth patterns of the congregation, and then presenting that information to the leadership.

Mike chose the latter course. He went to the men and asked them to work with him in evaluating the statistical information that was available. They found that one of the main factors in the growth of the congregation was a large influx of individuals into the community resulting from the establishment of two major factories within the last seven years. This immigration had slowed drastically, resulting in the growth rate of the congregation reverting to pre-development levels. In possession of this information, Mike and the men were able to present the facts to the rest of the leadership, and from this point they were able to develop new strategies to reach their community.

Factual conflicts are easily solved once all the information is gathered. An issue is or is not the case based on the realities at hand. Mike retreated from his initial feeling of seeing the concerns of the elders as personal criticism and chose the proper course of action by directing his attention toward what could be evaluated objectively.

Means conflicts concern themselves with the methods for dealing with a particular problem or carrying out a particular task. The problem may be accurately diagnosed, but the methods to be used to resolve the issue may themselves be a source of conflict. With good communication skills, this form of conflict has a high probability of resolution.

When we look at the conflict between the Hellenistic and Hebrew-speaking Jews in Acts 6, we see a conflict of means. Even though it is possible to see something sinister in the actions of those initially responsible for the food distribution, Luke does not indicate this in the text. The question that the apostles addressed was how to take care of this need in an efficient and responsible fashion. After communicating to the people the purpose that they believed God had called them to perform, the apostles proposed a method of dealing with the problem that satisfied all the parties concerned. The end result of dealing constructively with this conflict was the continued growth of the church.

Misunderstanding or confusion over the goals that a particular group or organization has may result in a conflict over ends. Many times it is assumed that everyone within the group understands the goal, the end being strived for, even though it has not been stated or presented in concrete form. When it becomes apparent that there is misunderstanding, conflict results.

John is the minister of a congregation in what was once a small, rural community located about thirty miles east of a large metropolitan area. Now the city has come to the country, and with the increase in population the congregation has experienced substantial growth. One might think that the result of that growth would be joy and excitement at the opportunity of seeing the Great Commission fulfilled in greater measure. Among many within the congregation, including John, this is exactly the case, but all is not well.

There are those within the congregation who are resentful of the newcomers. The status quo has been disrupted; old power structures are being threatened; and an entire new range of needs is being expressed, improved nursery facilities and new youth programs among them.

Obviously conflict exists or at best looms on the horizon, but what is it about? It is about goals or ends. Some in John's congregation have a goal of growth, reaching everyone in their community with the gospel of Christ. Others have the goal of keeping things the way they have always been, safely in a comfort zone, free from risks and uncertainties.

A final type of substantive conflict concerns values. Values are the foundation upon which goals and methods are built; they are the determining factor by which goals will be chosen and the means to accomplish them determined. Conflict resulting from different value systems is the most serious and difficult of conflict situations. Individuals will "shed blood" when basic values are at stake.

The primary issue faced by the Jerusalem council, the nature of salvation, was an issue of values. This issue would command the attention of the church for years following the council. It touched at the heart of the gospel and, as we saw in our evaluation of the biblical material, it promoted debates that were heated and vocally violent. Paul and Barnabas saw the attempt to Judaize the Gentiles as a threat to the very fabric of Christianity and were willing to go to any length, even to stand in opposition to the leaders of the Jerusalem church if need be, to maintain their position.

In any attempt to evaluate the nature and source of a particular conflict, not only must the objective facts of the conflict be taken into consideration but also the subjective factors of attitude, emotion, and communication. What may on the surface appear to be a conflict of method may have the force of a conflict of values because of the emotional commitment to the method that an individual possesses.

Over lunch Larry shared some of the struggles that he was going through as the minister of a congregation made up of a mixture of young professionals and retirees. After sharing much of the background of the congregation, he came to what he considered to be the focal point of the problem. Two of the younger members of the leadership had proposed the development of a mission statement for the congregation that would clearly state the reason for the congregation's existence and goals that could be developed out of this rationale. Immediate opposition to the proposal developed that was far stronger than was reasonable from several of the older leaders.

Larry's difficulty lay in understanding the basis for the opposition. He was being forced to mediate between two groups of leaders, both of whom he respected. While not seeing a mission statement as a total necessity, he did view it as a helpful tool for future growth and development. On the other hand, he saw men of great spiritual maturity reacting very strongly, causing him to wonder if there was something inherently wrong with the proposal that he had overlooked.

As we talked further, I asked Larry to think for a moment beyond the personalities involved—older versus younger, perceived maturity versus youthful enthusiasm—to the perception of each group toward the mission policy itself. The leaders had proposed the development of a mission statement as a means to an end, a method that would enable the leadership to orient itself in years to come. They believed that such a statement would aid the congregation to focus itself on ministry, to accomplish more for the glory of God.

Those in opposition to the mission statement had been in leadership for many years. They had experienced struggles in other congregations where loyalties to extra-biblical documents were stronger than loyalty to the Bible. Their opposition to the development of a mission statement apparently stemmed from what they perceived as a threat to a primary value, the authority of Scripture. They were apparently willing to go to the wall over this issue; hence the strong, almost unreasonable opposition.

As Larry came to see that the two groups were viewing the issue from two entirely different perspectives, he was able to return to the leaders and devise a strategy of intervention that led to resolution. He learned a very valuable lesson: a conflict can be viewed differently by groups or individuals. It is a must to determine the kind of conflict that is being engaged and to make sure that all parties are seeing the conflict from the same perspective.

HOW DO CONFLICTS DEVELOP?

Tension

The first session of the seminar had ended on a high note the previous evening. Of those attending, one couple, Mary and John, seemed eager to explore every aspect of the subject of conflict and were most perceptive in their questions and comments. I was excited for them because it was obvious that real growth in their lives was a possibility.

For Mary and John, the beginning of the second session the following night was anything but positive. Both seemed somewhat ill at ease, and in the course of the evening the tension between them seemed to grow. This couple that had been so involved in the previous evening's discussions were withdrawn, and if they made comments, they were somewhat sharp and derogatory if the spouse was the subject of the comment.

This young couple was exhibiting the first phase of conflict development, tension. The development of tension occurs at the beginning of any conflict at the point that an individual senses a loss of freedom within a relationship. This can be when one perceives that the goals being sought by another are mutually exclusive with his own or at the realization that one's needs collide with another's.

The real temptation at this point is to ignore personal goals or needs, to sweep the entire matter under the rug pretending that it does not exist. This can result from the feeling that the matter is so small that it is not worth confronting. Yet it is at this point that these tensions can most easily be handled. Misunderstandings can be corrected through open communication as well as the expression of needs and goals in order that both parties can achieve the desired end.

This tension may come from an even more simple explanation, which is stress. For all the negative press that stress has received, we need to be aware that stress is essential for life, as it provides

Figure 2.

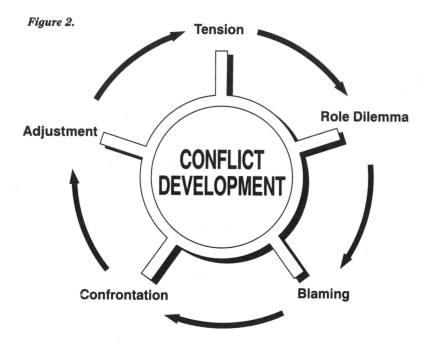

The illustration of the Conflict Cycle suggested by Jerry Robinson, Jr. and Roy A. Clifford, *Managing Conflict in Community Groups*, University of Illinois, 1974.

the motivating tension to deal with positive and negative events, tasks, and problems. Any circumstance in life can be a stressor and individuals will respond to the same set of stressors differently.

Four psychological reactions to stress have been identified by McSwain and Treadwell. First, strongly authoritarian individuals tend to handle new situations rigidly and with little doubt. These are most effective in assignments under stressful conditions. Second, individuals may externalize anger toward people or objects when stressed. Third, persons can internalize anger while being relatively nonauthoritarian in relationships, sensitive toward others, and flexible in adjusting to change. Finally, there are those who, when stressed, exhibit anxiety and frustration along with marked physical changes. This group is very sensitive toward others, is unable to relate authoritatively, and presents a lack of self-assurance.[3] The stress factor plays a major role in conflict. Stress will exist whenever there is change in circumstances, expectations, or goals. While many times in the background, in the initial stages of conflicts within the church, it may be a contributing factor to reactions that are observed. As conflicts develop, the ways that individuals consistently deal with stress will be seen more and more and must be taken into consideration as any resolution is attempted.

At the end of the seminar, both Mary and John came to the front of the room and asked if they could talk with me for a moment. John's words explained their reactions during the seminar. "The promotion that I have been waiting for for two years finally came through today. I was really excited about the challenge, the new ranges of authority, and of course the extra money. It can make a real difference to us. But we will have to relocate away from our families, friends, and of course the church. I really don't know if I will take it." This barrage of stress had created several points of tension. With the explanation came a release of the tension and we were able to talk through the situation, averting a major conflict in this young couple's life.

In reality, the point at which tension appears is the most crucial moment in the development of conflict. Conflict is easily dealt with at this point, but if tension is unnoticed or ignored the situation will move to the next stage of conflict development: the questioning of roles.

Questioning

Individuals who are in the second stage of role dilemma are questioning exactly what is going on in the situation. They are attempting to clarify their position as well as gain insight into the thinking of the opposing party. The feeling of tension that was present in the first stage can grow into a perception of being threatened. Communication that could have resolved the issue in the first stage becomes increasingly difficult as individuals begin to find support for their feelings or ideas.

Mark and Carrie had been married for two years when Mark came into the office. His face exhibited a great deal of tension and his hands, as they moved constantly, presented frustration and agitation. His conversation was full of question about his relationship with his wife. "What does she expect from me? Why is she acting this way? What else can I do?" Mark, a normally confident, self-assured young man, had come to the point of questioning his role within the marriage relationship. When I asked him about what had been occurring within their relationship, we uncovered several points of tension that had been ignored as unimportant on his part. These tensions had not disappeared but had led to further remarks on Carrie's part that underscored her need to have these frustrations resolved.

I encouraged Mark to initiate a conversation with Carrie that would explore these points of stress within their relationship and to find mutually acceptable solutions to them. This he did, and two weeks later both shared with me the renewed closeness they were experiencing that had been the initial mark of their relationship. If this difficulty had not been overcome, matters would have progressed to the third stage of conflict, injustice collecting.

Blaming

In this stage several dynamics are occurring. Individuals involved in the conflict pull apart, withdraw from one another. There is the tendency in this stage to begin the process of blaming, asserting that the total fault of the issue belongs to the other party.

It would have been very easy for Mark to have entered this stage in a full-blown way. When someone perceives that he is being attacked, the response of self-justification kicks in. There is always the tendency to view one's own self as innocent, providing ample justification for the responses offered. With a view of innocence in place, blame is attached to the other party or parties involved, with responsibility for the situation resting squarely on the shoulders of the "guilty."

In Christian organizations, virtues such as self-denial and humility are elevated above the satisfaction of having one's personal needs met. This concept is seen most in the example that Jesus set for his followers as he denied his own personal safety in going to the cross for the needs of others. In most conflict situations the primary issue, however, is that of needs. In many instances, those involved in conflict claim that they are in fact not arguing about needs or feelings but on the basis of Christian principles alone. The result is dehumanizing of conflict. The issue becomes then true faith versus false faith. Battle lines are drawn and ammunition is stored for the clash that will most certainly occur.

Frank had been an elder in the Brownwood church for a number of years, but recently (within the last two years) because of "job demands" had declined to serve. Because of his faithfulness and past willingness to serve, Frank was invited to serve on the Search Committee that was commissioned by the elders to seek out an individual to fill the staff position of Minister of Youth.

Over a three-month period of time, several meetings were held to develop the search process and to interview possible candidates. Frank was not able for various reasons to attend all of these meetings, but was updated by phone as to the progress that the committee was making. Unfortunately, Frank was away when the candidate that was ultimately presented was interviewed and a decision made to recommend him to the congregation.

At the congregational meeting called for the purpose of voting on the recommendation Frank made an impassioned speech that contained two primary accusations. He first accused the committee of ignoring his input, and second accused the eldership of lacking the spiritual maturity necessary to deal with what he perceived as problems that would be created by a multiple staff.

What had brought the Brownwood church to this point? In order to fully understand what was happening, it is necessary to go back to the years that Frank had served actively within the leadership of the church. During those years Frank had offered several suggestions as to policy and procedures. He felt that these were sound ideas but when many of these were not adopted or, as he thought, were "ignored," he became frustrated. Rather than express his frustration, he declined to serve because of his job responsibilities. The tensions in his life were not resolved and the role that he played within the leadership was never clarified. When the committee pushed on to carry out their commission, all of these feelings resurfaced and led to an outpouring of blame.

Confrontation

The fourth stage of conflict is that of confrontation. In this stage the activity involved can range from a simple clearing of the air to outright violence. These actions and all of those in between have occurred within the body of Christ. Confrontation is an uncomfortable but necessary time if individuals or groups are ever to reach their full potential. The issues that create tension will ultimately be confronted in some fashion. If confronted properly, the issues themselves will be the focus in the confrontation. If the issues are suppressed, ignored for a time and allowed to fester, the tendency is for individuals to be confronted, at times with disastrous results as in the case of the Brownwood church. The key to the outcome is in the area of management.

At our board meetings any member of the congregation is free to attend if he or she chooses. Rarely do we have nonboard members present merely to observe. They come usually with something to say. Such was the case about five years ago as a visitor shared his feeling that there was a conflict or a spirit of competition between our elders and deacons. An elder challenged the remarks as to their accuracy, but was immediately informed by one of our deacons that there was some basis for those feelings in his mind and in the minds of others present. The silence that followed was deafening.

This confrontation was unexpected as many are, with no opportunity to prepare a response or for realization that a response was needed. There did exist among this group a spirit of cooperation and a willingness to face the issues. A group of these men, myself included, was chosen to explore this issue; over the next six weeks we provided for the entire board an analysis of the problems we were facing and our recommendations as to ways of responding to them. The issues remained the focus of the discussions rather than people, and the result was a stronger group of leaders that have moved forward in their service to God. The key was a proper focus.

Adjustment

The final stage of conflict is adjustment. Conflict will produce change; the situation and the people involved will not remain static. When the confrontation phase of conflict is complete, individuals involved will either move forward in their service and devotion to God to a higher level of ministry, or they will find themselves in a disillusioned state of frustration where the stage is set for the conflict process to be repeated.

In this adjustment phase when conflict has been handled properly, several positives can result. A new sense of identity can occur when congregations face substantive issues and are forced to decide on their understanding of the mind of God in these matters. Groups that have been silent or uninvolved can become empowered by active participation in the decision-making process of the congregation. These same groups can also develop a cohesion with each other that increases loyalty to their purpose. Perseverance and staying power result as conflict is faced and resolved. More serious conflict is diffused as numerous people are involved in the process of conflict resolution before emotional factors emerge into destructive elements. As a result of conflict, more creative and satisfying feelings and solutions are desired.

Three negative results are immediately apparent when conflict is improperly handled or left unresolved. People are hurt. This is the most obvious of the negatives. Many times the hurt remains a major factor in their lives for many years to come. At times rigid structures are imposed to deal with future issues in the hopes that structure can insure that conflict will not happen. This rarely is successful. Finally, energy can be channeled into nonproductive or nonthreatening goals that rarely make a difference.

Conflict does not just happen. There are issues, small and great, in every conflict that should be addressed. When ignored or dealt with improperly, the result can be a seemingly never-ending roller coaster of events and confrontations that ultimately lead to disaster. An illustration of this can be seen in Fig. 3. When responded to adequately, the results can be productive and in the life of the church, growth and fulfillment of God's purpose can be the result.

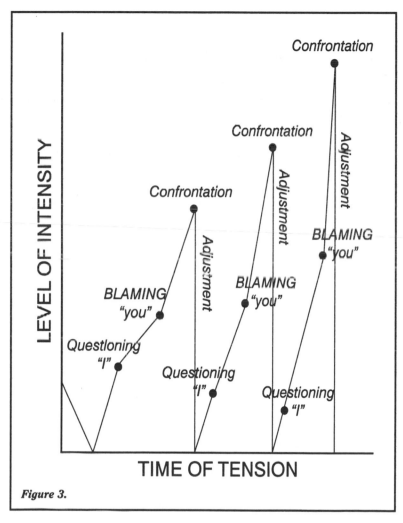

Figure 3.

In this model several dynamics are occurring. As conflict remains unresolved, the span of time between points of tension decreases. The questioning phase shortens, as the focus on self shifts to others, allowing movement to the blaming phase to quickly develop where the level of faultfinding rises. Confrontations intensify while the potential for permanent damage to relationships increases. The final phase of conflict, adjustment, is short-lived, as tension arises between the individuals again.

ENDNOTES

[1]William H. Willimon, *Preaching about Conflict in the Local Church* (Philadelphia: Westminster, 1987), p. 10.

[2]Jay Hall, *Conflict Management Survey* (The Woodlands: Teleometrics, 1986), p. 1.

[3]Larry L. McSwain and William C. Treadwell, Jr., *Conflict Ministry in the Church* (Nashville: Broadman, 1981), p. 53.

CHAPTER 5

HOW DO YOU MANAGE CONFLICT?

Each of us responds to conflict differently. Our response to conflict very well may be a product of learning, seeing others (especially our parents when we are young) respond to difficult situations in particular ways. Most of the time we are not aware that our response to conflict follows definite patterns, these patterns having become "old friends" that we have come to rely upon.

The following exercise is designed to obtain your response to twelve conflict situations. Kim Wigham, technical writer for Albany Technical Institute, has designed this self-analysis using a wide variety of situations both in and outside of the church. The point of this is to remind us that conflict does not exist only in a limited context but is a part of the fabric of life. There are no right or wrong responses.

The goal of the exercise is to promote awareness of how you respond to conflict as you record your response on the evaluation page at the end of the survey. Please follow the directions carefully as you proceed.

READ THESE DIRECTIONS
BEFORE PROCEEDING FURTHER

CIRCLE the letter of the response that best illustrates how you would respond. Do not answer based on how you feel you should respond but on the basis of what would be your normal reaction.

SITUATION NO. 1:

Your organization has shifted to a team management system. Now responsibilities are to be shared among employees. You are the team leader. One individual in your team refuses to cooperate with this new system of management. He does not like taking on responsibility or having to perform different jobs. He repeatedly complains and generally has a negative attitude. But, he is an essential member of your team.

You respond by: (circle one)

A. Ignoring the problem; sooner or later he will come around. If not, maybe your boss will take notice and handle the situation.

B. Allowing the team member to perform only the job he is comfortable with while you take up his duties in other areas.

C. Telling this member that he will have to learn all of the skills but that you will schedule his work to only include those he is comfortable with.

D. Telling the team member that either he will have to cooperate with this style of management and take on his job-related responsibilities or he will be fired.

E. Talking with and listening to the team member to discern the basis for his feelings. Then try to find a mutually agreeable solution.

SITUATION NO. 2:

The boss has recently asked you to take on some extra responsibilities not currently related to your position (and definitely below the general level). You are very busy putting together a package for him and do not have extra time to perform these duties.

You respond by: (circle one)

A. Allowing the work to just pile up. You'll take care of it when you get time.

B. Taking the extra duties and performing them. You decide to just catch up with your work after you complete his and, if necessary, take it home with you.

C. Telling your boss that you are willing to do some of the duties now but will have to handle the rest at a later date.

D. Telling your boss you are more than willing to perform the extra tasks he has assigned, but he will have to give you an extension on the package due at the end of the week.

E. Meeting with your boss, discussing your feelings about this situation, and trying to work out an arrangement in which you each get what you need without feeling "put upon."

SITUATION NO. 3:

Your company has recently implemented a new accounting system for your bookkeeping needs. This program is to be implemented into daily business by the end of the month. A co-worker versed in this program has been assigned (by your supervisor) to instruct you in this new system about which you have no prior knowledge. The deadline is less than two weeks away, and the co-worker assigned to instruct you has failed to set any time aside for training.

You would: (Circle one)

A. Decide to distance yourself from your boss so he cannot ask you how the training is going. Maybe if he does not see you, he will forget about the deadline for the accounting system's installation.

B. Keep your calendar relatively free so you will be available whenever the instructor can fit you into his schedule.

C. Go to your co-worker and suggest that you will come in an hour early and help him finish some outstanding work, if he will stay an hour late the next evening to instruct you.

D. Tell your co-worker that you want to start your training on Thursday (tomorrow). When he fails to agree to this date, you threaten to tell your supervisor how your co-worker has failed at this duty.

E. Approach your co-worker and give him a list of dates you are available for training. You request the same from him. From these lists the two of you choose a time which is convenient for both of you.

SITUATION NO. 4:

You are the chairman of the building and grounds ministry in your church. You have an important proposal to present to this evening's board meeting and the presentation is not complete. You are aware that there will be some opposition. John, a friend of yours, has stopped by your office just to pass the time of day.

You respond by: (circle one)

A. Welcoming John but not inviting him to sit down. You continue to work hoping he will take the hint and leave as quickly as possible.

B. Setting the work aside, and knowing that you will have to miss dinner, you invite John to come in because it has been several weeks since you have seen him.

C. Telling John that you only have about fifteen minutes that you can spare right now because of the proposal you are developing.

D. Telling John that he has come at a really bad time and because of the presentation, he will have to come back the next day.

E. Welcoming John and explaining the deadline that you are facing. You question him to see if there are any critical issues on his mind and, finding none, make an appointment for lunch the next day when you both can have more time.

SITUATION NO. 5:

You manage a shop that targets the fifty-year-old woman. There is an opening for a sales associate. Your cousin (she is 37) is qualified and experienced in this area but the home office has a policy prohibiting the hiring of family members. This position must be filled immediately and the only other applicant is an inexperienced, unqualified seventeen-year-old girl.

You would: (Circle one)

A. Ignore the policy and hire your cousin; maybe no one will notice.

B. Tell your cousin that you cannot hire her because the policy will not allow it.

C. Talk with the area manager about the policy. If they allow you to hire her, you will not work with her nor show any partiality to her.

D. Tell the area manager that your cousin is the person for the job and that you are going to hire her, especially since the other applicant is not qualified for the position.

E. Meet with your area manager. Explain the situation and why you want to hire your cousin. Find out the reason for this policy. With the area manager decide on an approach acceptable to both of you.

SITUATION NO. 6:

Sue has worked as the church secretary for one year. The last couple of months she has made several mistakes resulting in lost time, increased expense, and confusion within the congregation. Prior to this Sue was an outstanding employee. You discussed her performance with her a month ago and there has been no noticeable change.

You respond by: (Circle one)

A. Continuing to ignore her sloppy work. Sooner or later she will quit and then you can hire someone else.

B. Editing all of her work before anything is finalized. Everyone has a hard time; she will change.

C. Talking with Sue. Offer to give her a half day off if she will reduce her errors.

D. Firing Sue. She is not doing her work.

E. Meeting with Sue again. Find the reason for her poor workmanship. Discuss mutual needs and search for a way to achieve your goals.

SITUATION NO. 7:

One of your fellow employees is always telling off-color jokes. You do not appreciate this, nor do some of the other employees.

You respond by: (Circle one)

A. Not paying any attention. Perhaps if you do not acknowledge his remarks, he will stop making them.

B. Reminding the other employees that he is only human and that we have all told stories like this at one time or another.

C. Talking with this person and asking him not to make his off-color remarks while in your presence.

D. Telling this person that you do not like his remarks. If he does not stop making them, you will go to your supervisor and file a formal complaint.

E. Talking with this person and explaining your feelings regarding his remarks. Discuss some ways to allow you both to be yourselves without offending the other.

SITUATION NO. 8:

You are currently developing a new training manual for your company. It is to be sent to the publisher in one week. Although it has been approved by the information expert, the team leader has decided it is not thorough enough. He has requested that you gather additional information and rewrite fifteen of the twenty previously approved chapters while maintaining the same deadline.

You respond by: (Circle one)

A. Going ahead and sending it to the publisher. The team leader probably won't ever look at this manual again.

B. Reorganizing your total work schedule and canceling meetings so you can meet the team leader's needs within the deadline.

C. Calling the team leader and telling him you will be glad to add the additional information, but you will have to extend the deadline by 3 weeks.

D. Telling the team leader you will not add provide additional information since the manual had already been approved by the information expert.

E. Talking with the team leader and finding out what his needs are. Explain your situation to him and then decide on a suitable solution to meet both of your needs.

SITUATION NO. 9:

As youth coordinator you have the task of working with two volunteers (John and Mary) whose combined talents greatly enhance your program. John is very job specific and feels threatened by Mary's abilities and suggestions. Mary is willing to share her expertise and responsibilities but senses that John is resentful of her.

You respond by: (Circle one)

A. Deciding to ignore this situation. Your department has made achievements in the past and will continue to do so.

B. Continuing to give John specific duties while acting as a go-between to combine his talents with Mary's.

C. Telling John that he is to try to work with Mary but that you will limit their shared responsibilities.

D. Telling John that he must work with Mary and if he cannot do this you will have to find a replacement.

E. Talking with John to discuss his feelings about working with Mary, developing a list of needs, and seeking a solution that would meet those needs.

SITUATION NO. 10:

Your company has recently switched to a team management approach. (You are the plant manager.) Several individuals have applied for an opening within your plant. All of the applications are reviewed by the team. The team has chosen an individual whom you feel will be ineffective in fulfilling the requirements of the open position.

You respond by: (Circle one)

A. Deciding to wait a week before making any definite decision; maybe the guy will find another job.

B. Deciding to go ahead and hire the individual since you implemented the "Team" philosophy with your employees.

C. Telling the team they can hire him, but that they will be responsible for any mistakes made by him.

D. Telling the team that you will not hire this individual. You have more experience in this area and know he will not fulfill your plant's needs.

E. Holding an open forum meeting during which everyone explains his view. Decide on a path to follow which will allow all of you to find an individual with the desired qualities.

SITUATION NO. 11:

John is continuously late for work by 30-45 minutes. Once he arrives, though, he attends to all his duties and is very helpful both to you and to others. The company has no tolerance for unexcused tardiness. When John is late his duties fall into your lap. John's tardiness has increased from once a week to an average of three.

You respond by: (Circle one)

A. Ignoring the behavior. You know he will get caught sooner or later.

B. Continuing to cover for John by taking on more of his duties. You know he has a lot going on in his life right now, and everyone needs help.

C. Telling John you will continue to cover for him, but you will need him to cover for you one or two afternoons a week.

D. Telling John you are not going to take care of his responsibilities anymore, because when you do that, you get behind in your own duties.

E. Talking to John about ways in which both of you can accomplish your duties at work without hindering the other. Recommend he talk with the employer about changing his scheduled work time.

SITUATION NO. 12:

One of your friends is manipulating large amounts of your time. He is having a very difficult time at home which is creating difficulties in all areas of his life. His calls during work hours have put you behind, causing your manager to raise questions about your effectiveness.

You respond by: (Circle one)

A. Having your secretary screen your calls and instructing her to tell this person that you are out of the office. Hopefully he will get the hint.

B. Continuing to listen to his concerns and ideas; keep reassuring him that he is moving in the right direction. He is in reality a friend in need.

C. Telling him that you will give him an hour of your time once a week after hours but in the meantime he will have to cease calling you on the job.

D. Telling him that you have heard this all before and that you have said all that you can say. He must get on with his life and allow you to get on with yours.

E. Meeting with your friend for the purpose of explaining to him the situation that you are facing with your manager. Explain that you understand his need for a friend but also point out that he may need a higher quality of help than you are equipped to give. Work together to maintain your relationship and also move on toward a greater effectiveness.

Please go to the next page and score the survey.

Review the responses that you circled and count the number of A's, B's, C's, etc., that you have. In the chart below record the number of times that you responded with each letter.

A's Avoidance
B's Accommodation
C's Compromise
D's Competing
E's Collaborating

In the chart below list in descending order, greatest to least, the categories based on the number of times you selected that category.

Categories	# Responses

CHAPTER 6

INTERPRETING THE SCORES AND STYLES

WHAT DO THE SCORES MEAN?

Having taken several self-analysis instruments over the last few years, I found myself, following their completion, asking predominantly the same questions each time. "Why were some of the situations similar? Why should I have had difficulty choosing between some of the responses? I could just as easily have chosen one of the others. What do the scores mean?" Perhaps you have had much the same reaction. In response to your questions, let me give you the responses that I have received.

First of all, no instrument is perfect. They are designed to record general reactions to general situations. An individual is encouraged to pick the response that is closest to the one that would actually be done. While it may be very close it will, in all probability, not match perfectly. However, the pattern that is established will give an individual a fairly accurate assessment of how he does respond to particular situations.

Second, some of the situations are similar because life carries with it some similarities. Individuals who have similar jobs, interests, or activities have to deal with like situations. Also, in any given occupation or activity, certain types of situations are reoccurring. Yes, there may be slight variations but a pattern can be discerned.

Finally, as to the scores in this survey, several things should be noted. Individuals have a preferred style of conflict management, the category with the highest score. This is the style that is used initially when conflict arises, the one that the individual has found to be more successful or is most comfortable in using.

This primary style is supplemented by a second and possibly a third backup style. You have noted those styles with the second and third highest scores. If the primary style of conflict management is not successfully employed, the others will be used as the conflict intensifies.

Upon taking the survey I scored eight in collaboration, two in compromising, and one in competing. Generally when conflict arises I follow just such a process in my attempts to resolve an issue.

You may have noticed in recording your scores that you scored fairly evenly in several areas without one style being dominant over the rest. Individuals who test out in this fashion have discovered a wide variety of conflict management skills and use them accordingly. This is a balanced approach that allows for flexibility in dealing with issues. Most of us do not possess this wide a variety of flexibility.

In order to grasp then how these styles are applied, let's look at them individually.

THE CONFLICT STYLES

Individuals have identified five basic styles or ways that conflict is handled, whether in or out of the church. (For a more complete discussion of these styles, see Shawchuck, *How to Manage Conflict in the Church*, 21-27; Lewis, *Resolving Church Conflicts*, 76-78; McSwain and Treadwell, *Conflict Ministry in the Church*, 170-182; Leas, *A Lay Person's Guide to Conflict Management*, 10-11; Hall, *Conflict Management Survey*, 16-17; and Vale and Hughes, *Getting Even*, 40-44.) While different terms are applied at times by different authors, for the purpose of this study, the five styles will be labeled avoidance, accommodation, compromise, competition, and collaboration.

Avoidance

Pessimism and hopelessness characterize the avoidance style of conflict management. An individual who consistently practices this style feels that it is not possible to accomplish his goals in a conflict situation. The basic strategy becomes to withdraw or get away from conflict whenever possible. The expectation of losing is always present, and rather than undergo such a frustration, the person "exits stage right."

Not only are individual goals sacrificed on the altar of avoidance, but relationships are set aside as well. No support will be offered to individuals as they attempt to define the conflict or seek and carry out solutions to it. The person becomes a detached observer who is willing to forgo a positive contribution to the relationship in return for noninvolvement.

Those who consistently practice this style may leave a situation psychologically as well as withdraw physically. If they do remain in a situation, the result will be compliance without commitment and an accumulation of feelings of frustration, weakness, and ultimately deep hostility. This hostility may very well erupt at an inappropriate time with great intensity.

Frank, the former elder of the Brownwood church, is an example of one who practices avoidance. In the times where he felt that his ideas were rejected, he avoided confronting the rejection and discovering exactly what was happening. In doing that he suppressed his own goals, ultimately leaving the eldership rather than running the risk of further rejection.

These feelings, however, did not disappear. They continued to build until he responded with a series of accusations that allowed him to vent his frustrations but still not deal with the real issue that was involved. This venting itself could be viewed as avoidance because it was directed at others and did not address the primary problem.

Ultimately a consistent practice of avoidance produces a no-win situation for those who become involved in a relationship with one who uses this as his preferred style of conflict management. Everyone loses, as issues are not resolved because one or more of the participants absent themselves from the conflict. Feelings can be trampled inadvertently because no one is aware that a conflict exists. To be sure there are some conflicts that should be avoided, times that one should distance himself from situations. However, a consistent practice of avoidance can be unhealthy for all involved.

Accommodation

Len felt that he was one of the luckiest guys around. He couldn't understand how he had managed to attract Donna and ultimately marry her. Having come from a background where his parents were divorced, he had observed firsthand some of the problems that afflict families. He had vowed that he would do whatever was necessary to preserve the relationship he had with Donna.

Now four years into the marriage he was beginning to feel the first pangs of resentment. He had tried to be a good husband, providing everything necessary for his family. He had gone beyond the necessities, providing the resources to enable them to have a very comfortable life.

Emotionally Len had sacrificed himself as well. Remembering the demanding, selfish approach to life used by his father, which had been a major factor in his parents' divorce, Len did not assert himself in any major way in any of the discussions he had with Donna. Even when he knew he was correct and subsequent events supported his feelings, he allowed Donna to have her way, feeling that it was better to give in for the sake of the relationship rather than press his own views.

This second style of conflict management is called accommodation, which is characterized by a high concern for preserving relationships rather than accomplishing goals. The individual using this style will be basically passive in conflicts that concern him but quite active in assisting others as they work through their particular conflict situation. The person using this style assumes that relationships are so fragile that they cannot tolerate serious conflict and, therefore, will give up pressing for his goals in order to reduce the threat that the conflict poses to the relationship. The message communicated is one of sacrifice for the good and benefit of the other person, and in reality one loses everything while the other party wins all.

As noble as this style may appear to be on the surface, there are some serious liabilities that come with its consistent use. First of all, the individual using this style may ignore personal needs of self-support because he is so concerned for the care and support of others. Second, for the individual who is accommodated in the relationship, there is the tendency to become more aggressive in the relationship, feeling vindicated by the passivity of the partner. His demands may increase. Finally, the cost to the user is cumulative, making the burden of the relationship very great.

There are circumstances where the style of accommodation is very valuable and useful to preserve relationships or unity within a group. This is especially true when the issues at stake are not goals or values but deal primarily with methodology. One method may be as good as another, and to relinquish our adherence to a particular method for the preservation of a relationship or unity within a congregation can be a very effective style of conflict management.

Compromise

In this style of conflict management, each party of the conflict wins and loses something as a solution to the conflict. It is based on the premise that it is impossible for everyone to be fully satisfied but desirable to continue in the relationship for the good of the organization. Compromise is most effective where the differences are attitudinal or based in feelings. If the issues are more substantive and are held with deep emotion, compromise will be more difficult.

Even though this style of conflict management has been touted as the most effective means of dealing with problems, there are shortcomings. In reality, skepticism can be a real side effect of the consistent use of this style. When consistently goals are never fully

realized and relationships are always developed around the bargain-
ing table, the end result is value confusion and a climate of suspicion.

Hank worked in mid-level management in a rural community in
the midwest. The plant in which he worked had had a long history
of labor disputes that affected the economy of the entire area as
many of the individuals in three counties worked there for their
primary source of employment and farmed as a side line. The opera-
tion seemed always under the threat of closure by its parent
company in the east.

As a member of the labor relations board, Hank found himself
constantly having to make deal and effect compromises with union
and management officials alike in order to keep down costs and to
raise productivity. In Hank's words, "I feel like Monty Hall on 'Let's
Make a Deal.' What's the least I have to give up in order to get the
most from you?" Hank's attitude was one of suspicion, always looking for the catch, constantly looking for hidden motives and agen-
das.

Hank brought that same style of conflict management with him
as he served on the church board of a medium-sized congregation.
For the most part the style worked effectively. However, as time
passed he began to react to his fellow board members with the same
levels of suspicion and motive examination used at the plant.

Following a rather heated exchange between Hank and another
board member, one of the older men pulled Hank off to the side and
gently began to probe for the source of the feelings he had exhibited. Very quickly the older man sensed that Hank was viewing the
conflict as if it were a management/labor dispute necessitating the
losing of some ground in order to gain as much as possible.

Since the issue under discussion was the establishment of goals
and directions for the Sunday School, he reminded Hank that both
parties were striving for the same end—growth—and that very possibly neither would have to give up anything in order to accomplish
his task. With that in mind, Hank discovered that it was not necessary to respond to each conflict in the same way. He also realized

that not every participant in conflict was as covert as some with whom he had to deal, and that he could approach issues without constantly looking for something hidden underneath the issue being discussed.

Competition

The intent of this style is always to win. Only two results of conflict are viewed possible: winning and losing. Since everyone realizes that winning is always better than losing, the end result is high fulfillment of personal goals and devastated relationships. The competitor sees his own self-worth tied to every issue, and to be worthwhile or successful he must win. The approach to conflict management becomes aggressive, inflexible, and unreasonable.

A competitor gets things accomplished as he usually has a clear idea of what needs to be done and how to do it. He is very willing to get involved in an issue, especially if it directly affects the accomplishment of a personal goal. One might say that these individuals are driven in that they focus their energies directly on the problem until it is resolved.

There is a price to be paid, however, for the consistent use of competition as a style of conflict management. Relationships are easily damaged or destroyed as a result of its habitual use. Even if those involved acquiesce to the wishes and goals of the competitor, an undercurrent of resentment and anger may develop that will surface at a later date.

A further price to be paid may be in the lack of ownership and support that a group has toward the idea that the competitor wishes to implement. Tasks may go unfinished or not taken seriously. The competitor in turn may become more aggressive, driving the group harder, leading to a much larger confrontation.

Tom describes himself as a very up-front person. "This is what I am like and I am not going to change very much for anyone. People can pretty much take or leave it; it really doesn't matter to me."

Tom is a competitor and a lonely and frustrated one at that. The trail of his life is littered with the "bodies" of those who have attempted to disagree with him. For years Tom has wondered why he has not been able to hold good employees. Now Tom faces the question of why his wife and children are gone and he just cannot understand. To be sure this is an extreme example, but it points out the dangers of this style being used to excess.

Collaboration

Collaboration combines a high concern for the accomplishing of one's goals with an equally high concern for the relationship that is affected by the conflict. The two are not seen as mutually exclusive, and, in fact, the person using a collaborating style believes that all goals must be served if the relationship is to endure.

This style is best used when all parties are esteemed as persons of value. It is based in the assumption that individuals are capable of confronting differences without being personally hurt or hurting the relationship. It has a high tolerance for differences and works to promote a climate of trust and openness, recognizing that feelings are legitimate. A failure of communication concerning the possibility of mutually compatible goals is seen as the main issue.

The gathering of apostles and other leaders of the church as recorded in Acts 15 is an excellent example of a collaborative style of conflict management. There existed on Paul's part a high concern for the primary issue involved, the basis of salvation being either in the law or the grace of Christ. On the part of James there was the concern for individuals, how not to offend Jewish Christians while accepting the Gentiles on the basis of grace in Christ.

Even though this was an emotionally charged issue felt critically by all parties involved, there existed a willingness to work toward a solution that would satisfy all parties while maintaining a commitment to the truth. While many issues that involve high levels of emotion are often beyond this type of problem solving, there were sufficient levels of commitment to enable the groups involved to remain focused until a solution could be reached.

The disadvantage to the method is that not all conflicts lend themselves to this type of technique. Certain situations because of time constraints require more direct forms of action. Settings in which factions of a group adopt mutually exclusive goals are often beyond this method. Not every individual possesses the level of maturity required of this method.

HOW DO THESE STYLES WORK?

As has been stated, each individual has a preferred style of conflict management. This is the style that is used most consistently in conflict situations. This style is chosen over a period of time as individuals observe parents, teachers, or other respected individuals handle conflict. Other factors, such as teaching contexts or individual study and involvement in conflict itself, provide selection opportunities. In other words, conflict styles are learned styles.

As important as the preferred style are those secondary styles which come into play less frequently. As an individual enters a conflict situation initially, the preferred style will be used. If the use of this preferred style does not provide the desired results, the secondary or back-up styles will then be used. Not only the preferred but also the secondary styles are available as responses to conflict. These are selected and ordered according to our interpretations of conflict.

In the long run the collaborating style of conflict management is to be preferred. By nature and practice, it allows for the greatest amount of goal achievement while preserving the relationships necessary to accomplish tasks. Even if this is not the preferred style at the present time, individuals can learn to respond to situations in a different manner. Old, less-productive patterns can be unlearned, so that a style more appropriate to the situation can be applied.

Another point needs to be made. At certain points all of these styles can be valid and useful responses to certain conflicts. A manager may use a competing style when a quick decision needs to be made and time is not available for prolonged discussion. Avoidance may be useful when the issue is not vital. Accommodation can be the appropriate response when the preservation of a relationship is so vital that the issue can be relinquished.

In the next section an attempt will be made to bring the concepts learned in the first four sections to bear on the life of the church as it experiences conflict in its attempt to minister.

CHAPTER 7
WHEN THE LINE IS CROSSED

Before we go any further in our discussion, let's go back to the playground illustration at the beginning of the book. Children can be great teachers, and perhaps we might observe in them some of the things about which we have been talking.

Obviously their conflict began the moment one sensed that he had been wronged by the other breaking in front of him. The conflict quickly escalated into a conflict of values over which they were willing to shed blood, preferably the other person's. They both used a competitive style of conflict management initially but fell back on a collaborative style upon intervention by the school authorities.

These two boys would frown with little understanding if this were explained to them. Perhaps this same reaction occurred when we began this discussion of conflict management because we believed that conflict simply was an issue of personalities. However, we have learned that there are many dynamics involved, and in order to comprehend what is happening in conflict these dynamics must be understood.

Any attempt to resolve conflict requires that individuals or leadership, if they are acting in a third-party role, understand what basic assumptions about conflict are at work in the situation. Is conflict assumed to be sinful? Have individuals "spiritualized" their goals to escalate the conflict into a "true faith" versus "false faith" situation? What conflict styles are at work in the situation? Have the real issues been lost and replaced by emotions? At what stage of the conflict process are the individuals? What does the Bible commit us to in the area of conflict? These kinds of questions must be asked if there is to be resolution. The leadership of congregations can well serve their people by discussing these types of questions before any issue surfaces.

Individuals need to learn to recognize conflict at its earliest stage. Many conflicts that have resulted in explosions could have been successfully handled at the initial point of tension. In all relationships individuals need to develop a sensitivity that is alert, perceiving when tension is developing and being responsive to dealing with the issue at hand.

Leaders should also evaluate the potential for conflict that exists in any given situation. As a part of this evaluation, these kinds of questions need to be asked. 1) What kinds of conflict have been a part of this congregation's life? 2) What were the results of those conflicts? 3) Does the organizational structure of the congregation lend itself to conflict? What personal and structural relationships exist within the congregation? What stresses are at work within the congregation at the present time? Each answer will enable the leadership to gauge the conflict potential that exists within the group. It is best to find the answers to these questions prior to a conflict occurring, when there is calm and a large measure of rationality and sensitivity.

Even with this kind of evaluation taking place, there will be those times when conflict occurs, erupting at times with monumental proportions. If the above questions have been asked and answered, then individuals and leaders will have the necessary background to proceed, and proceed they must, but where and how?

SEVEN-STEP PROCESS

In the next sections a procedure is offered for engaging and resolving conflict in order that the sometimes disastrous results of conflict can be avoided. At the outset it must be said that this procedure is neither foolproof nor guaranteed to produce peace and harmony. Some situations are beyond that. It does, however, offer a method and a measure of hope that encourage movement beyond initial paralysis and frustration.

Step 1: Avoid with Integrity

The first step of the procedure may seem at first contradictory with the tone set in previous chapters. The consistent practice of avoidance as a means of conflict resolution is unhealthy for all the parties involved. In this context the operative emphasis is on the phrase "with integrity." What do we mean to avoid with integrity?

In situations where emotions have already erupted, provide the opportunity for the parties involved to withdraw from the field with integrity. In essence call a time out. Allow enough time to pass before engagement is resumed to allow the individuals to reflect upon the situation at hand and to approach the issue with clarity of thinking. Set a time frame for further engagement and use this time to gain as much information as possible concerning the background and nature of the conflict, the maturity level of those engaged, and the emotional temperature of those involved.

Following the emotionally charged congregational meeting at the Brownwood church, Robert, the minister, made a very wise move. Rather than setting up a meeting with the elders immediately, he calmly approached the chairman requesting a meeting for the end of the week. In the course of the week, he assured those in leadership that this conflict could be resolved and asked probing questions to attempt to find as much background about Frank and his feelings as possible.

As the week progressed, he was able to discern a pattern in Frank's behavior, not only in church life but also with his family and work responsibilities. This pattern presented a habitual use of avoidance whenever conflict arose, and Robert assumed correctly that when Frank could no longer use this style he had reverted to his secondary style of competition.

At the end of the week when the elders met, a different attitude was present than that observed at the conclusion of the congregational meeting. While still upset over the situation, the explosive anger that had been present was no longer in evidence. The predominant feeling was one of concern for the candidate who had been put on hold, for the congregation which was highly confused, and for Frank that his hurt might be healed. This week of avoidance with integrity had served to bring a calm and rational spirit to the ones who would have to ultimately work to resolve the conflict.

The period of time allocated for this step will be different in each instance. The person working to resolve a given conflict must learn to rely upon the Spirit of God and his understanding of the situation to help in determining the length of time before re-engagement is attempted. One must also be careful not to convey that what is really being done with this time is a shelving of the issue, a sweeping of the conflict under the carpet.

At times the circumstances make this step almost impossible to achieve. Attitudes, the involvement of individuals with a competitive style, the heightened emotional level of those engaged in conflict, and the nature of the very issues themselves can serve to lesson the amount of "AWI" available. Make every effort to preserve this time; its value is exceptional.

Step 2: Communicate Correct Information

After having collected all the information available concerning the problem that is at the root of the conflict, communicate your understanding of the issues involved. This must be done as clearly as possible with all of those individuals who are a part of the conflict. The best method is to make notes and distribute them to those involved. These notes should include information concerning the history of the conflict (has it been avoided in the past and has raised its head again from under the carpet); how the conflict is being viewed, e.g., some view the issue as method while others see it as a values issue; and where the conflict is occurring in the conflict cycle.

In doing this, those individuals engaged in conflict must be given three things. First, individuals must be given permission to disagree without feeling guilty. Any attempt on the part of others to attach guilt to differences of opinion must be resisted. Second, individuals must be given the opportunity to state their position with strength and clarity. In the beginning stages of conflict resolution, guidelines must be put into place that give the procedure of the resolution and ensure that individuals will be heard without fear of interruption, ridicule, or emotional put-downs. Individuals must be convinced that they can deal with the issue at hand and can solve it productively. Third, protection must be granted to those who are willing to take the emotional risk of dealing with the conflict. Again, this can be accomplished in the initial stages of resolution.

Following the confrontation in our board meeting involving an alleged division between our elders and deacons, the group that was chosen to resolve the issues met several times for discussion. In the initial meeting I encouraged them to be open and honest with their feelings about the nature of the problems we were facing. We established guidelines concerning how these sessions were to be conducted, ensuring that everyone would be given a hearing without fear of retaliation. We established a reporting process where notes were taken at each meeting, then copied and distributed not only to the members of the group but to other board members as well.

This informative process took time, but it enabled every member of the group to be aware of what had been discussed and any decisions that had been made as a result of that discussion. It also kept the process "up front" for those members of the board not involved in the actual resolution process. No one had to wonder if his viewpoint was being heard or if something clandestine was occurring. A real sense of confidence in the process developed.

Step 3: Find Areas of Agreement

Point out those areas where there is agreement. Many times individuals feel totally alienated without that being the case at all. Helping them to see that there are mutual beliefs and goals will bring them closer together and will help them to identify the base upon which a future relationship and accomplishment of goals can be reached.

My dad made a keen observation about our minister following a morning worship service. He said, "You can always tell when there is a problem in the church. Gene begins preaching on the love that we share in Jesus Christ." Not every sermon that our minister preached on the subject of love occurred because of a problem, but my dad did realize that Gene was pointing out the basic common denominator that was shared by everyone in the congregation.

Even though the differences that people have between one another possess substance, when the content of those differences is disclosed, it is best to show in verbal or written form the commonalities that inherently exist between them. Many times it is just those commonalities that provide the basis for moving on in the process and give hope for an eventual resolution.

Step 4: Examine Differences of Opinion

Following a rehearsal of the facts of the issues involved and a sharing of the common things agreed upon between individuals or groups, there may be fewer areas to be negotiated than once thought. With the individuals providing their input, develop a list of all the options that are available for solving the issue. Individuals must be given the opportunity to see and evaluate the options available and how these would work out in the particular situation.

Many times at this point in the resolution process, I will have the individuals involved respond in written form to eight questions. The first four serve as a review tool to cause the participants to go over in their minds exactly what has happened. The second four direct the individuals to look forward to enable them to clearly formulate in their minds what they would like to see happen from this point. The questions are:

1. What do I think the problem is about?
2. What does he/she think the problem is about?

3. How did I contribute to the problem?
4. How did he/she contribute to the problem?
5. What do I want done about the problem?
6. What does he/she want done about the problem?
7. What will I do about the problem?
8. What will he/she do about the problem?

The answers to these questions will enable the next step to move forward naturally.

Step 5: Develop a Consensus

Individuals involved in conflict tend to see a problem as having only one solution. In reality there may be several options available that will satisfy the need of the moment. For those involved in the resolution process, it is vital that these options be brought to light and evaluated.

Leaders must constantly keep the goals of individuals in tension with the relationships shared by them. To do this leaders must enable the individuals to work toward solutions that not only accomplish the primary goals but also enable the relationships to be preserved.

Individuals tend to support and promote those solutions that they have helped create. A solution that is forced upon an individual or group which they do not "own" will ultimately be no solution at all and may serve to enlarge the problem. As has been stated before, a collaborating style of conflict management best serves this process.

Recently I conducted a conflict management seminar for one of our local companies which has adopted a team concept as its management style. This management style allows for and, in fact, encourages the collaborative style. However, as the seminar progressed I became aware of an undercurrent of tension that caused me to wonder exactly what was going on. About midway through the first day I found out.

At the second break the Operations Manager and another employee were involved in a conversation, and I overheard the manager say, "I have the position and I have the power that goes with it! What I say goes!" The employee's response was a definite, "Yes, sir!"

Even though the official policy stated that the plant would operate as a team, here was evidence to the contrary. Whatever the issue was under discussion, the solution was certainly not owned by the individual affected. He would "under protest" go along with the Ops Manager's decision, but I could not help but wonder when further conflict would develop.

Participants should review the answers to the questions asked in the previous section. These answers should provide the needed material out of which can come several alternatives to the problem. As these are explored, people can be encouraged to find those that are mutually agreeable and get the job done.

In the discussions concerning the supposed division between our elders and deacons, the problem that was finally exposed was the absence of concrete goals for our congregation. When this finally hit home, the resolution group began to focus on the development of realistic, attainable goals that could be striven for by the leadership and congregation. Many were suggested, some were rejected, and all were refined so that there was group ownership of the objectives presented to the full leadership group. No votes were taken; unity was the goal, and it was reached.

Step 6: Celebrate the Resolution

When workable solutions have been selected that meet the personal needs of the individuals involved, there should be a time of celebration. This can be as simple as a handshake or a strong hug, or in the case of conflict that has involved the entire congregation, a time of communion that emphasizes the unity of the body of Christ.

This step in the process should not be minimized because it is an opportunity to affirm the power of God to work in all kinds of situations. People need to be reminded that God does work in all things to bring about good to his people. It should serve to excite individuals about the possibilities of the future, to develop a heightened sense of group unity. It should also be used to remind folk of what has been learned and to encourage them to respond more positively when conflict comes again, as it will.

Step 7: Check Back on the Situation

It is necessary to conduct a review of how the solutions are working. There should be a definite timetable in place prior to celebration to assure individuals that checks will be made. This enables them to have confidence that things will not have to progress the same distance as before in order to achieve relief. Also, knowledge of future reviews motivates individuals to honestly work at the solution.

Each year in January our leadership goes away for a two-day planning conference. We use this as our primary check-up time to make sure that we are on track with our stated goals. It also serves as a time when old objectives are revised and new ones are developed. In doing this, frustrations are aired and victories celebrated in an atmosphere of acceptance and accountability.

Conflicts are never resolved unless patterns of behavior are changed. The tensions that created the conflict in the beginning will remain. The honesty of follow-up should ensure that when conflict comes again, it will not be derived from the same source.

Floyd Strater shared this story several years ago concerning a congregation that invited him to conduct a revival meeting in their community. At the beginning of the meeting he was approached at separate times by two individuals. Each of the individuals stated that he was sure he saw that the congregation was one afflicted by a major conflict. They both encouraged him to speak out in favor of their side of the issue, feeling confident that he would recognize the validity of their side.

The issue was one of those monumental ones like the color of carpet in the fellowship hall, or whether the lights in the sanctuary should be round or rectangle. Even though we might laugh, if we are honest, each of us has been involved in conflicts where the issues were similar and those involved elevated them to a test of true spirituality.

As preachers are prone to do, Floyd was wandering around the building the following day. He looked into the baptistry and, rather than water, found an overflow of broken chairs and tables, outdated Sunday School material, and other assorted castoffs. It was obvious that the baptistry had not been used for some time for its intended purpose. The conflict that appeared rather harmless had paralyzed the life and ministry of this congregation.

Rather than calling a meeting of the leadership to discuss the issue, Floyd began one of the most creative resolutions I have ever heard of. He went to each of the principal leaders of the factions involved and invited them and their following to a meeting at the church that afternoon for the purpose of resolving the issue. He also visited the local hardware store, purchased several items of cleaning equipment, and settled back to await the arrival of the congregation.

At the appointed hour, the cars began arriving and as the individuals walked from the parking lot to the building, it was obvious that there was surprise and tension on the faces of everyone. Floyd reminded them of their common faith, their common task of reaching their community with the gospel, and their common desire, evidenced by the contacts of the two leaders, to resolve this difficulty. He then led them to the baptistry area, gave them the materials he had purchased, and waited.

Most of the group had not realized the condition of the facility, but as they viewed the pitiful state of affairs, they came to realize that their conflict had played a large part in bringing them to this point.

Throughout the afternoon they labored, and as the time passed a difference in attitude began to be seen and felt. Individuals who for many months had only spoken to each other with extreme politeness now began to talk; two men who had not been able to work together on anything began hauling trash away; and laughter was again heard in the building. The issue that had divided them was put in its proper perspective and resolved.

During the remainder of the week the congregation experienced a real measure of renewal. As the purpose and task of the congregation were brought into focus, they began to move beyond the issue that had divided them toward the growth that each one desired.

In this intervention, steps one and two are taken for granted. There had been avoidance with integrity and information about the conflict was common knowledge. There was not open hostility and everyone knew the nature of the issue. The key to this intervention was to focus on the common ground that the groups possessed, and when the issue was seen in the light of this, resolution quickly came about. The remainder of the week became a celebration of that resolution and hopefully, even though information is not available, there have been checks in the life of the congregation to see that things are working properly.

Where do we go from here?

CHAPTER 8

LOOKING AHEAD

As we look toward the future, we might hope to see a life filled with relationships that are free from all forms of conflict. Yet it seems to me that as long as we have children and playgrounds, and adults in relationships, we will have conflict from time to time. A life free from conflict might be attractive, but I am convinced that God uses conflict to teach us things that possibly cannot be learned from any other source.

During one of the seminars that I was conducting, a lady remarked, "It seems that you must really enjoy conflict." Her comment startled me and caused me to think for a few moments before I replied. "No, I do not especially enjoy conflict," I said, "but I do believe that God has done some wonderful things in the lives of individuals and in the life of his church as folks have honestly attempted to deal with their differences."

It is for that very reason that I remain hopeful in the midst of conflict. I anticipate what God is trying to teach me about myself, others, or himself. He may want me to learn that there is another way to accomplish a task. He may desire to teach me about the values that others possess. God may display his power to bring about change that I have thought improbable.

I look for what God can do as the result of his people responding to conflict in a biblical fashion. In each of the conflict chapters in the book of Acts, Luke closes out his narrative of these events with the statement that growth occurred. The growth may have been in the numbers of disciples, in the qualitative spiritual growth of believers, or in the strength and power of the Word of God.

Each conflict that erupts in a relationship is a cause for concern. Innocent people can be hurt, one can experience a range of tension that is almost maddening, or sinful behavior can occur which can destroy fellowship. If a variety of conflicts are occurring and the rate and intensity of these are increasing, immediate attention should be given to resolving the issues at hand before disaster occurs.

Conflict is never fun, but it possesses great potential. To be sure there is the potential for evil, but there is also a great potential for good to occur. If a line is drawn and someone dares to step across, do not despair. Sin in all probability has not occurred. Work with the people and the issues involved to find a solution that allows God to be praised. We may even be prompted to say, "It was worth it all. See what God has done."

REFERENCE LIST

PRIMARY SOURCES
Books

Anderson, Ray S. *Minding God's Business*. Grand Rapids: William B. Eerdmans, 1986.

Bauer, Walter. *A Greek-English Lexicon of the New Testament*. Translated by William F. Arndt and F. Wilbur Gingrich. Chicago: University of Chicago Press, 1968.

Blanchard, Kenneth, Patricia Zigarmi, and Drea Zigarmi. *Leadership and the One Minute Manager*. New York: William Morrow, 1985.

Bossart, Donald E. *Creative Conflict in Religious Education and Church Administration*. Birmingham: Religious Education, 1980.

Bruce, F.F. *Commentary on the Book of Acts*. Grand Rapids: William B. Eerdmans, 1968.

Carson, D.A. *Matthew*. Edited by Frank E. Gaebelein. Vol. 8, *Expositor's Bible Commentary*, Grand Rapids: Zondervan, 1984.

Clinton, J. Robert. *The Making of a Leader*. Colorado Springs: Navpress, 1988.

Delitzsch, F. *Isaiah*. Translated by James Martin. Grand Rapids: William B. Eerdmans, 1976.

Fenton, Horace L., Jr. *When Christians Clash: How to Prevent and Resolve the Pain of Conflict*. Downers Grove: InterVarsity, 1987.

Flynn, Leslie B. *When the Saints Come Marching In*. Wheaton: Victor, 1988.

Gray, George Buchanan. *The Book of Isaiah*. Edinburgh: T. & T. Clark, 1928.

Hall, Jay. *Conflict Management Survey*. The Woodlands: Teleometrics, 1986.

Hersey, Paul, and Kenneth H. Blanchard. *Management of Organizational Behavior.* Englewood Cliffs: Prentice Hall, 1972.

Kittlaus, Paul, and Speed B. Leas. *Church Fights.* Philadelphia: Westminster, 1973.

Laney, J. Carl. *A Guide to Church Discipline.* Minneapolis: Bethany House, 1985.

Leas, Speed B. *A Lay Person's Guide to Conflict Management.* Washington: The Alban Institute, 1979.

_____. *Leadership and Conflict.* Nashville: Abingdon, 1982.

Lindgren, Alvin J., and Norman Shawchuck. *Management for Your Church.* Nashville: Abingdon, 1977.

Longenecker, Richard N. *Acts.* Edited by Frank E. Gaebelein. Vol. 9, *Expostitor's Bible Commentary.* Grand Rapids: Zondervan, 1981.

McSwain, Larry L., and William C. Treadwell, Jr. *Conflict Ministry in the Church.* Nashville: Broadman, 1981.

Peters, Tom, and Nancy Austin. *A Passion for Excellence.* New York: Random House, 1985.

Rush, Myron. *Management: A Biblical Approach.* Wheaton: Victor, 1987.

Russell, Bob. *Making Things Happen.* Cincinnati: Standard, 1987.

Shawchuck, Norman. *How to Manage Conflict in the Church.* Indianapolis: Spiritual Growth Resources, 1983.

Shelley, Marshall. *Well-Intentioned Dragons: Ministering to Problem People in the Church,* Vol. 1. Waco: Word, 1985.

Wagner, C. Peter. *Leading Your Church to Growth.* Ventura: Regal, 1984.

Wessell, Walter W. *Mark.* Edited by Frank E. Gaebelein. Vol. 8, *Expositor's Bible Commentary.* Philadelphia: Westminster, 1984.

Willimon, William H. *Preaching About Conflict in the Local Church.* Philadelphia: Westminster, 1987.

Articles

Schneider, Johannes. "συζητεω," in *Theological Dictionary of the New Testament,* Vol. 7, ed. Gerhard Friedrich. Translated by Geoffrey W. Bromiley. Grand Rapids: William B. Eerdmans, 1971.

_____. "ζητησις," in *Theological Dictionary of the New Testament.* Vol. 2, ed. Gerhard Kittel. Translated by Geoffry W. Bromiley. Grand Rapids: William B. Eerdmans, 1964.

SECONDARY SOURCES

Books

Argyris, Chris. *Management and Organizational Development.* New York: McGraw-Hill, 1971.

Augsberger, David W. *Caring Enough to Confront.* Glendale: Regal, 1973.

_____. *Caring Enough to Forgive/Caring Enough to Not Forgive.* Ventura: Regal, 1981.

Dale, Robert D. *Surviving Difficult Church Members.* Nashville: Abingdon, 1984.

Dudley, Carl S., and Earle Hilgert. *New Testament Tensions and the Contemporary Church.* Fortress, 1987.

Harkness, Georgia. *The Ministry of Reconciliation.* Nashville: Abingdon, 1971.

Huttenlocker, Keith. *Conflict and Caring.* Grand Rapids: Zondervan, 1988.

Janis, Irving L., and Leon Mann. *Decision Making: A Psychological Analysis of Conflict, Choice, and Commitment.* New York: Free, 1977.

Leas, Speed B. *"Should the Pastor Be Fired?" How to Deal Constructively with Clergy-Lay Conflict.* Washington: The Alban Institute, 1980.

Lewis, Douglass. *Resolving Church Conflicts.* San Francisco: Harper & Row, 1981.

Marshall, I. Howard. *Luke: Historian and Theologian.* Grand Rapids: Zondervan, 1971.

Robbins, Stephen P. *Managing Organizational Conflict.* Englewood Cliffs: Prentice-Hall, 1974.

Roth, Gustave, Norman Shawchuck, and Karen Stoyanoff. *Fundamentals of Evaluation.* Downers Grove: Organizational Resources, 1979.

Schaller, Lyle E. *Survival Tactics in the Parish.* Nashville: Abingdon, 1977.

Smedes, Lewis B. *Forgive and Forget.* San Francisco: Harper & Row, 1984.

Vale, John W., and Robert B. Hughes. *Getting Even: Handling Conflict So That Both Sides Win.* Grand Rapids: Zondervan, 1987.

Walton, Richard E. *Interpersonal Peacemaking: Confrontations and Third Party Consultation.* Reading: Addison-Wesley, 1969.

Articles

Banashek, Mary-Ellen. "Office Arguments: How to Clash With Class." *Mademoiselle* (September, 1986): 144.

Bertrand, K. "Negotiating Win-Win Solutions." *Business Marketing* 72 (July, 1987): 42.

Greenhalgh, L. "Managing Conflict." *Sloan Managment Review* 27 (Summer, 1986): 45-51.

Morgan, P.I. "Resolving Conflict Through Win-Win Negotiating." *Management Solutions* 32 (August, 1987): 4-10.

Prein, H. "Strategies for Third Party Intervention." *Human Relations* 40 (November, 1987): 699-719.

Watkins, Karen. "When Co-Workers Clash." *Training and Development Journal* 40 (April, 1986): 26-27.

Wilcox, J.R. et. al. "Communicating Creatively in Conflict Situations." *Management Solutions* 31 (October, 1986): 18-24.

RECOMMENDED READINGS

Books

Amstutz, Mark R. *An Introduction to Political Science: The Management of Conflict.* Glenview: Scott, Foresman, 1982.

Anderson, James D., and Ezra Earl Jones. *The Management of Ministry.* New York: Harper & Row, 1978.

Axelrod, Robert. *The Evolution of Cooperation.* New York: Basic, 1984.

Bagby, Daniel. *Understanding Anger in the Church.* Nashville: Broadman, 1979.

Berne, Eric. *Games People Play: The Psychology of Human Relationships.* New York: Grove, 1967.

Bramson, Robert M. *Coping With Difficult People.* New York: Ballantine, 1981.

Campbell, David. *If I'm in Charge Here, Why Is Everybody Laughing?* Niles: Argus, 1980.

Cartwright, Desmond S., and Carol I. Cartwright. *Psychological Adjustment: Behavior and the Inner World.* Chicago: Rand McNally, 1971.

Collins, Randall. *Conflict Sociology: Toward an Explanatory Science.* New York: Academic Press, 1975.

Deutsch, Morton. *The Resolution of Conflict: Constructive and Destructive Processes.* New Haven: Yale University Press, 1973.

Dittes, James E. *When the People Say No: Conflict and the Call to Ministry.* San Francisco: Harper & Row, 1979.

Filley, Alan. *Interpersonal Conflict Resolution.* Glenview: Scott, Foresman, 1975.

Friedman, Edwin H. *Generation to Generation.* New York: Guilford, 1985.

Hadden, Jeffrey K. *The Gathering Storm in the Churches: A Sociologist's View of the Widening Gap Between Clergy and Laymen.* New York: Doubleday, 1969.

Keating, Charles J. *Dealing With Difficult People.* Ramsey: Paulist, 1984.

Likert, Rensis, and Jane Gibson. *New Ways of Managing Conflict.* New York: McGraw-Hill, 1976.

Mahl, George F. *Psychological Conflict and Defense.* Chicago: Harcourt Brace Jovanovich, 1971.

McCarty, Doran C. *Working With People.* Nashville: Broadman, 1986.

Mickey, Paul A., and Robert L. Wilson. *Conflict and Resolution.* Nashville: Abingdon, 1973.

Miller, John M. *The Contentious Community: Constructive Conflict in the Church.* Philadelphia: Westminster, 1978.

Muck, Terry. *When to Take a Risk.* Waco: Word, 1987.

Palazzoli, Mara Selvini. *The Hidden Games of Organizations.* New York: Random House, 1986.

Rackham, Richard Betward. *The Acts of the Apostles.* Grand Rapids: Baker Book House, 1964.

Schmidt, Paul F. *Coping With Difficult People.* Philadelphia: Westminster, 1980.

Stagner, Ross, comp. *The Dimensions of Human Conflict.* Detroit: Wayne State University Press, 1967.

Articles

Caffarella, Rosemary S. "Managing Conflict: An Analytical Tool." *Training and Development Journal* 38 (February, 1984): 34-38.

Carter, J. "How to Handle Disagreement." *Managing Solutions* 32 (Summer, 1987): 27-33.

Chasnoff, Robert, and Peter Muniz. "Training to Manage Conflicts."

Training and Development Journal 39 (January, 1985): 49-53.

Coleman, James S. "Social Cleavage and Religious Conflict." *The Journal of Social Issues* 12, 1956: 44-56.

Coombs, Clyde H. "The Structure of Conflict." *American Psychologist* 42 (April, 1987): 355-363.

Crouch, Andrew G., and Philip Yetton. "Manager Behavior, Leadership Style, and Subordinate Performance: An Empirical Extension of the Vroom-Yetton Conflict Rule." *Organizational Behavior and Human Decision Processes* 39 (June, 1987): 384-396.

Curran, Dolores. "Family Fights Don't Have to Be Fatal." *U.S. Catholic* 52 (September, 1987): 22.

Dewey, Edith A. "Adlerian Principles in Conflict Resolution." *Individual Psychology: Journal of Adlerian Theory, Research and Practice* 41 (June, 1985): 237-242.

Dittes, James E. "To Accept and Celebrate Conflict." *Ministry Studies* (December, 1968): 43-46.

Donnelly, Doris. "Forgiveness and Recidivism." *Pastoral Psychology* 33 (Fall, 1984): 15-24.

Fisher, Roger. "Dealing With Conflict Among Individuals and Nations: Are There Common Principles?" *Psychoanalytical Inquiry* 6, 1986: 143-153.

Fogg, R.W. "Dealing With Conflict: A Repertoire of Creative, Peaceful Approaches." *Conflict Resolutions* 29 (June, 1985): 330-358.

Gordon, Bonnie. "Settling Conflicts Among Your Workers." *Nation's Business* (March, 1988): 70.

Jarvis, Peter. "The Ministry-Laity Relationship: A Case of Potential Conflict." *Sociological Analysis* 37, 1976: 74-80.

Kelly, James R. "Escaping the Dilemma: Reconciliation and a Communication Model of Conflict." *Review of Religious Research* 19 (Winter, 1978): 166-177.

Kolb, D.M., and P.A. Glidden. "Getting to Know Your Conflict Options." *Personal Administration* 31 (June, 1986): 77-78.

Lally, John, Jr. "A Theology of Conflict." *Commonwealth* 86 (December, 1967): 355-358.

Latham, Tony. "Violence in the Family: An Attempt to Apply Contemporary Theories of Non-Violent Action and Conflict Resolution Skills." *Journal of Family Therapy* 8 (May, 1986): 125-137.

Morley, Donald D., and Pamela Shockley-Zalabak. "Conflict Avoiders and Compromisers: Toward an Understanding of Their Organizational Communication Style." *Group and Organization Studies* 11 (December, 1986): 387-402.

Schein, Edgar H. "Improving Face-to-Face Relationships." *Sloan Management Review Portfolio: The Art of Managing Change and Uncertainty, Sloan Management Review,* 1983

Sternberg, R.J., and L.J. Soriano. "Styles of Conflict Resolution." *Personal Social Psychology* 47 (July, 1984): 115-126.

Volkema, Roger J. "Training Disputants: Theory and Practice." *Mediation Quarterly* (Fall, 1986): 43-52.

Warehime, Robert G., and Danny R. Lowe. "Assessing Assertiveness in Work Settings: A Discrimination Measure." *Psychological Reports* 53 (December, 1983): 1007-1012.

Wilson, James A. "Winners and Losers: Knowing the Difference Between Them." *Organization Development Journal* 3 (Summer, 1985): 39-40.